Praise for *Find the Helpers*

"Hopefully, this book will move you, upset you, enrage you, and, ultimately, inspire you to be the best 'Helper' you can be. Because life is so much better for those who are helped AND for those who do the helping. Fred suffered the ultimate loss and chose to turn it into the ultimate mission: to protect our children from gun violence. As a career homicide prosecutor, I had the unimaginable privilege of working with hundreds of 'homicide families.' No family should ever have to bear that horrific label. Yet once a family suffers the loss of a loved one to violent crime, some feel that the label 'homicide family' will forever define them. Fred is living proof that we need not be defined by our darkest day. In his painful yet ultimately uplifting memoir, Fred Guttenberg is a living tribute to the triumph of purpose over tragedy. And he has helped us all."

—Glenn Kirschner, Legal Analyst and Former US
Army prosecutor

"If you're looking to discover the best of us during the worst of times, read Fred Guttenberg's *Find the Helpers*. Fred shares his journey of unimaginable grief at losing his brother to a 9/11-related illness and his daughter at Parkland. Yet, from Fred's loss, we read about his strength to not only find the helpers around him, but to become one to others."

—Congressman Eric Swalwell

"Fred Guttenberg's life with his family before Valentine's Day 2018 sounds almost magical. He had two wonderful children, a loving wife, a successful track record as a businessman, and he lived in Parkland, Florida, a community considered one of the safest in the nation. That all changed on Feb. 14, 2018, when his daughter Jaime was killed in her classroom along with sixteen other students and teachers. Like so many others who are survivors of gun violence, there was Fred's life before losing Jaime and Fred's life afterward. This book talks about his life afterward, but in doing so it affirms something much bigger. This book is so important because it lifts up the essential role of 'helpers'—friends, neighbors, fellow advocates, elected officials, and even strangers—without whom real change, and the energy necessary to be a change agent, would be impossible. In the disconnected, now socially isolated world in which we live, Fred reaffirms the central importance of real human connection, often at the most random moments, that can make the difference between marching on or giving up. As I write this, our nation is experiencing an awakening of consciousness to profoundly disturbing issues. I hope all who want to make a change in this world for the better read this amazing book and understand how 'helpers' made a difference in Fred's life and how every one of us has a role in creating the change we want to see in the world. Simply being a 'helper' can be the secret ingredient, the catalyst, for the real and sustaining changes needed to make our world a better and safer place for everyone."

—Kris Brown, President of Brady

"We each have something to learn from Fred Guttenberg. Amid heartbreaking loss, Fred has found reason to press forward. In *Find the Helpers*, Fred shares of finding support and comfort from those he knew and those he had not yet met, a journey that would lead him to friendships with the Vice President and with the Speaker of the House. And he shares of his enduring commitment to ending gun violence through dogged and tireless advocacy. Fred once shared with me that he wished he had started the work to end gun violence before it was too late for him and his family. His lesson is now ours. His words now our calling."

—Former Congressman David Jolly

"No one should experience what Fred Guttenberg has, not once but twice. Fred has taken searing loss and made it a mission. His story is extraordinary, perhaps all the more so because he didn't seek anything more than a good life for his loved ones, a simple, ordinary happiness and togetherness. Fred Guttenberg is a dad and brother whose deep love for his family was put to the test by the crucible of grief, shock, and pain. He took that and turned it into a passion for taking a stand and making a difference. May you be inspired by Fred's book *Find the Helpers*. I know I am."

—Alyssa Milano

"Fred Guttenberg has lived through the unimaginable. The shooting death of his beautiful daughter Jaime in Parkland was reported all over the world. It is impossible to know the anguish that Fred carries after such a catastrophic loss, but because of this beautiful book, we are shown the way toward hope, belief in the good of humanity, and discovering purpose. Through his story we meet all the Helpers who helped carry his pain when he couldn't, and we see Fred, now strong and focused, a fierce leader and compassionate Helper."

—Debra Messing

"Few people better exemplify the power of turning tragedy into action than Fred Guttenberg. His grace, resilience, and courage in the face of unspeakable heartbreak serve as inspiration to us all. In the fight to end gun violence in America, Fred has not only been there for me, but has also found ways to engage new voices and build new bridges while honoring the memory of his daughter. This book offers powerful and heartening lessons on how we can help one another move forward and build a safer, more just world."

—Former Congresswoman Gabby Giffords

FIND

THE

HELPERS

FIND THE HELPERS

What 9/11 and Parkland Taught Me about

Recovery, Purpose, and Hope

Fred Guttenberg

Mango Publishing
CORAL GABLES

Cover Design: Gabi Mechaber
Layout & Design: Gabi Mechaber

For permission requests, please contact the publisher at:
Mango Publishing Group
2850 S Douglas Road, 2nd Floor
Coral Gables, FL 33134 USA
info@mango.bz

For special orders, quantity sales, course adoptions and corporate sales, please email the publisher at sales@mango.bz. For trade and wholesale sales, please contact Ingram Publisher Services at customer.service@ingramcontent.com or +1.800.509.4887.

Find the Helpers: What 9/11 and Parkland Taught Me about Recovery, Purpose, and Hope

Library of Congress Cataloging-in-Publication number: 2020940929
ISBN: (print) 978-1-64250-535-1, (ebook) 978-1-64250-536-8
BISAC category code BISAC: BIO032000—BIOGRAPHY & AUTOBIOGRAPHY/ Social Activists

Printed in the United States of America

To all victims of gun violence and all who grieve a loss.

Table of Contents

Foreword

"Unconfirmed reports of a school shooting coming out of Parkland, Florida, this morning…"

I heard it on my car radio on February 14, 2018. Valentine's Day.

It was early in Los Angeles. I cursed the dashboard and raced through the perverse calculus every parent goes through when they hear this news in the age of normalized mass shootings. Maybe the report was wrong. Or maybe the shooter would be apprehended without casualties. Or maybe just one kid was killed or injured. Or maybe just a couple of kids. Because that would be better. Just a few lives snuffed out, just a few families' capacity to experience unmitigated joy obliterated forever by a sorrow that is permanent and deep.

When I got home, I turned the TV on and saw that, yet again, wishful thinking was no match for a country that can't muster the political will to protect its own children from being executed in their classrooms with weapons of war.

I saw the scores of ambulances. The desperate parents, shaking with fear, waiting to find out if they were about to experience the greatest relief of their lives or to be summoned to hear the words that no human being should ever have to hear.

The weirdness of a beautiful day desecrated. The horror of a beautiful school, just hours ago brimming with hope and energy and flirting and smiles, reduced to a slaughterhouse.

I got angry at the somber tones of the correspondents and the public officials who spoke, because I knew that "thoughts and prayers" were all the victims and their families were going to get. The news cycle would move on. It always moved on.

The NRA, having morphed from the nonpartisan gun safety group I knew as a kid to a partisan firearms manufacturers' lobby and apparent money laundering operation for the Russians, would continue its sway over our elected officials. They would continue to deny the common sense gun safety regulations that the vast majority of the country understand are necessary.

Nothing would get done.

After all, two years earlier, forty-nine people were slaughtered at the Pulse nightclub.

Nothing got done.

Six years earlier at Sandy Hook Elementary School, a disturbed man, legally armed to the teeth, shot and killed twenty-six people, including twenty children between the ages of six and seven and six adult staff members.

Nothing got done.

Later, our president would stoop to revel in the endorsement of a conspiracy theorist who desecrated the memories of the victims at Sandy Hook with the contemptable lie that the massacre never even happened. That it had been staged by a cabal of liberal "crisis actors" hellbent on undermining our constitutional rights. The bereft parents of the lost children would be harassed for their complicity in the supposed hoax. The innocent children blown apart by a weapon designed to inflict maximum casualties on the battlefield were not the victims. The NRA was.

In fact, the more catastrophic the loss of life, the stronger the NRA's grip on our dysfunctional political system seemed to get. And with each tragedy, gun profiteers were rewarded with a rise in sales of their lethal, irresponsibly marketed products, ensuring that the deadly cycle of violence would not only continue, but grow.

And grow it did. Mass shootings spiked in 2017. School shootings were no longer aberrations. They were expected. It occurred to me that perhaps the most obscene thing about the Parkland Massacre was that it was predictable. We were waiting for it.

As the coverage turned to the victims, in the litany of shattered innocence and dreams, I saw a beautiful picture of a dark-haired girl flying through the air, beaming.

"Jaime Guttenberg," the anchor intoned, "she was a dancer."

I knew that girl. A dark-haired girl who lit up the room when she danced? I knew her. I turned off the TV and called my daughter, a nineteen-year-old dancer who was studying in Chicago.

I needed to hear her voice.

In the days and weeks and months and years that have followed, the Marjory Stoneman Douglas community has refused to allow us to accept the absurd notion that the blood of our children is the cost of freedom.

Something would get done.

The young people would make sure of it.

Just three days after the shooting, I was struck by the fearlessness and clarity of Emma Gonzalez as she called out the NRA and the politicians it owns with the refrain "We call BS!" Delaney Tarr. David Hogg. Cameron Kasky. The articulate grace under pressure of all the Never Again MSD and March for Our Lives kids was mind-boggling to me. There was something shameful about the fact that kids so recently traumatized should have to be the ones thrust into the media spotlight to fight a battle my generation should have won decades ago.

But they are up to the task.

I started clocking Jaime's father, Fred Guttenberg, in interviews and events following the shooting. At first, I could feel him gasping through his grief as if he might drown in despair. But I could feel his outrage grow after Donald Trump lied to his face about standing up to the NRA. And I could feel his resolve stiffen as the enormity and the moral bankruptcy of what he was up against revealed itself.

Soon he seemed to adopt the mantra of the great John Lewis, that when we are confronted with injustice, we must be willing to get into trouble: good trouble, necessary trouble. There he was at the Kavanaugh hearing, shunned as he tried to shake the nominee's hand. I cheered when his inability to contain his outrage in the face of Trump's lies got him kicked out of the State of the Union address.

Fred Guttenberg is one of those rarest of human beings who, as they endure the unimaginable, have the strength to see beyond their own suffering. They hear a call to action to do whatever they can to alleviate that suffering in others and, in doing so, hold this country up to its spectacular, unfulfilled promise. They understand that politics is the way we create our moral vision. They know that despair is a luxury the future cannot afford. And that action is the antidote to despair.

Fred Guttenberg inspires me every day as a citizen and as an activist. But more than anything, I'm inspired by Fred's example as a father—a loving, heroic dad who, as long as he is here and no matter what obstacles he faces, will fight to make sure that his daughter's voice is heard.

BRADLEY WHITFORD

Introduction

On a Day of Love

Hanging with Jaime during a family vacation in New York

My mother used to say, a long time ago, whenever there would be any real catastrophe in the movies or on the air, 'Always look for the helpers. There will always be helpers.' That's why I think if news programs could make a conscious effort of showing rescue teams, medical people, anyone coming into a place of tragedy, to be sure that they include that. Because if you look for the helpers, you'll know there's hope."

—Fred Rogers, interview with Television Academy, 1999

It's true what they say: Grief is love with no place to go. When you lose someone or something, you have all these feelings that no longer have a destination. The feelings just seep out of you like air in a drafty house.

To get by, you have to find people to help you. You have to find your helpers. They will be the fuel to keep you going, the spark to get you started again. Thankfully, I have had many helpers in what I call my crazy new life, some more unexpected than others. How else can I explain what happened on the evening of February 14, 2020? On this day, it had been exactly two years since my daughter was murdered.

We had some family and friends at our home helping my wife, Jennifer, my son, Jesse, and me get through this day. Around 6 p.m., I headed to the local pizzeria to get food for everyone. As I was pulling out of the driveway, my phone rang. It was Vice President Joe Biden. He was calling for nothing more than to check in on my wife, my son, and me, and to let us know he was thinking of us on this day.

I have often spoken of my relationship with the Vice President and how much his advice and counsel have meant to me, even back before he was the Democratic nominee for the presidency. On that day, this call had great significance.

For me, the Vice President has been a helper. He has truly given me the advice that I needed to go forward from the worst moment in my life, often speaking to me about mission and purpose. That advice has formed my life and my advocacy since. Now, in addition to being a helper, he is also potentially the future President of the United States.

February 14, 2018, was supposed to be a day of love. Instead of a romantic dinner with my wife, the plan was to watch our wedding video with our fourteen-year-old daughter and sixteen-year-old son as a way of showing them the beauty of Valentine's Day. My daughter Jaime had come up with the idea.

Our family drill that morning started off like any other day. The kids were running late for school, the dogs were barking because they wanted to be fed and walked, and Jennifer and I were scrambling to get ready for work. These are the details I remember from that morning. What I cannot remember still haunts me. I can't recall if I told my kids I loved them as they ran out the door. I was too busy telling them, "You're late! You need to get to school." I never expected these would be my final words to my daughter.

Thirty-four people were shot that day at Marjory Stoneman Douglas High School in Parkland, Florida, with seventeen killed and seventeen injured. My daughter Jaime, a tough-as-nails fourteen-year-old dancer with a huge heart, was the second-to-last victim to be shot. The shooter had gone to the third floor—where Jaime was—with the intention of shooting students on that floor and those outside through a window. While the shooter was reloading his AR-15, she took off down the hallway toward the stairwell. Authorities think she was maybe one foot away from turning the corner. One foot away from safety. One foot that would have allowed her to join up with her older brother, Jesse, at a nearby Walmart, and then to make her way back to her mother's and my arms.

At the time of Jaime's death, I was already struggling with deep personal loss. Just four months earlier, my brother Michael died of pancreatic cancer due to complications from his service on 9/11. He had been exposed to so much dust and chemicals while working to help out at Ground Zero that, in the end, the damage caught up with him. Michael battled his cancer heroically for nearly five years, passing away at age fifty.

Grief is unpredictable. You milk those good days and then do whatever you must to get through the bad ones. The day of the most recent State of the Union speech turned into a day that was both good and bad. As the guest of the Speaker of the House, Nancy Pelosi, for the second year in a row, I sat in the House of Representatives chamber listening to Donald Trump talk about the violent threat of illegal immigrants. I wanted to yell out that the person who killed my daughter was an American, not an immigrant. So when he followed up by saying he was going to protect the Second Amendment, and all the Republicans in the room got on their feet to cheer, I lost it. My unexpected outburst got me handcuffed and detained by the Capitol Police. That was the bad part of the day.

But there was a good part, too. When I was released from detention the night of the State of the Union speech, Speaker Pelosi's staff were waiting to take me back to my hotel. One of them told me Speaker Pelosi would be calling shortly. *Oh no,* I thought.

When the speaker got on the phone with me, I apologized profusely to her for causing a scene. She brushed it off. "Nonsense," she said. "Don't you ever stop speaking out, Fred." Her compassion for me that night after I'd been detained was just enough to keep me going.

Find the helpers. They will assist you in ways you can't imagine and don't expect. They don't have to be high-powered politicians like Pelosi or people with great wealth. They can be your loved ones, your family members, your neighbors, your colleagues, people from your church or temple congregation, or even total strangers. Whatever hardship you're going through, you can't get through it alone. The night Jaime was killed, her dance sisters made orange ribbons in her memory—orange was Jaime's favorite color. That was an inspiration in itself, but then a picture of the young women wearing their ribbons went viral on social media. Within twenty-four hours, people all around the dance world were wearing orange ribbons. A Los Angeles-area mom came up with the idea of the dancers wearing orange ribbons at their competitions. Professional dancers at the American Ballet Theatre posted on Instagram showing orange ribbons affixed to their costumes. Broadway shows like *The Lion King* and *Hamilton* honored Jaime by wearing orange ribbons. Seeing all of this support for Jaime helped us get through that rough first week—and inspired us to start her foundation, Orange Ribbons for Jaime.

Jen McGuire, a news writer for Romper.com, beautifully covered the orange ribbon tribute: "All over the country this weekend, people will be dancing for Jaime. She'll be present in auditoriums, in concert halls, in theaters, and dance studios. The memory of Jaime Guttenberg and the senseless violence that cut her life so terribly short will spread through the country, one orange ribbon at a time. It's a lovely tribute, one her family might appreciate through the terrible fog of their own crippling grief. Wearing an orange ribbon for Jaime will keep her memory alive, even as her family plans her funeral. Because I guess that's the cold, awful reality, isn't it?"

In February 2020, days after the two-year mark of our loss, we held a fundraiser, and three comedians—Jessica Kirson, Jim Breuer, and Alonzo Bodden—volunteered their time to raise money for our cause. Everyone who attended said that they had not laughed like that in years—including me and my family. Being able to laugh with our loved ones, our friends, and our community was a healing moment that will not be forgotten: more helpers from unexpected places.

This book is not about gun safety or what happened at Parkland. Instead, I share the story of the journey I've been on since Jaime's death and how I've been able to get through the worst of times thanks to the love and kindness of others. I tell the story of my family life, my brother Michael's illness and untimely death, and the story of what happened to my family and our community. Despite these very hard subjects, this book looks forward. You need to know, despite how hard it's been, *I got this*. What's more, **You** *got this*.

I know what it's like—you turn on the TV or open social media and maybe all you want to do sometimes is crawl under the covers. But hang on and look past the noise. You can get through these moments when they happen, whatever the moments in your life may be, as long as you look for the helpers. So much of what I've learned these past few years boils down to how amazing and decent people are. I have been truly touched by those I've known for years, those I have gotten to know, people in media, and people in politics—and the extent of their thoughtfulness and compassion.

I'm just a guy who grew up on Long Island listening to Billy Joel. I worked my butt off for years at Johnson & Johnson and then as a Dunkin' Donuts franchise owner so that I could enjoy a quiet life with my wife and two beautiful kids. Now I'm in the public spotlight. I have a quarter of a million Twitter followers and am on TV all the time. I did not ask to be in this position, yet here I am.

In his famous book, Rabbi Harold S. Kushner wrote about when bad things happen to good people; my book focuses on when good things happen to good people at the hands of other good

people. Because one thing I've learned in the past two years
is that the world is filled with them. They include everyone
from the amazing gun violence survivors whom I have met in
communities around the country to the former Vice President of
the United States. They include people ranging from the former
Republican governor John Kasich, who encouraged me to restore
my faith in God (to be honest, I'm still working on it), to the
Florida Panthers NHL hockey team I worked with to organize
an anniversary event. They include a wealthy Republican donor
who was so fed up with gun violence that he reached out to me
and taught me about fighting for your beliefs. They are my two
best friends from childhood, both of whom rushed to my side—
one by plane, one by car—as soon as they heard the news of the
shooting, and relatives who did the same. Then there were the
countless other people, celebrities and strangers, who did not have
to go out of their way to show their love, but they did—because
that's what good people do.

These days, the quality time I spend with my daughter is at a
cemetery, sitting on a bench, either looking at her gravestone
or staring out into the distance at a lake with a fountain in
the middle. People who see me there—and I go there often—
probably think I'm nuts, because I have full conversations with
her. I tell her about the family, about things going on in my life;
all the same stuff I would have told her if she were sitting on the
couch with me watching TV. When the weather is good, I often
sit on my bench and look up at the sky for some sign that we're
all connected to the universe.

When I leave the cemetery, I continue a ritual I've always had
with my daughter and the rest of my family in which we kiss
each other three times whenever we're saying goodbye. It's just
something we made up and have always done since the kids were
little. I've been a cheesy sentimental dad all of their lives, and

fortunately, they put up with it, even into their teenage years. When it's time to say goodbye to Jaime, I kneel down and kiss her headstone three times. *Until next time.*

My life goes on.

But when we lost Jaime, I wasn't so sure it would. The day after the shooting, there was a vigil in Parkland, broadcast live on national TV. Jen decided to stay home, but I went with Jesse, other family members, and friends. The mayor of Parkland asked me to speak in front of the audience. I didn't know what to say, but when I took the microphone, I spoke from the heart. I told the world how I had rushed my kids out the door that morning because they were running late, and how I was troubled, not knowing if I told my daughter I loved her.

"I don't know what I do next," I said.

Now I do.

My personal mission is to break the gun lobby. My goal for the rest of my life is to help elect every government official who supports gun safety laws and to campaign against anyone who doesn't. But I have a separate mission for this book. To fight, you have to have hope. And this book is about nourishing the soul so that you have the stamina to fight. This book is meant to be a beacon of love and hope and compassion. Combined with my advocacy, my hope is that it will finally shift an unmovable object.

Finally, I want this book to be a message about perspective and perseverance. When your challenging moment comes, how you react to it and the attitude you choose to have in response will help define you going forward. I especially want to inspire young people by providing examples of what advocacy and direct action look like. I want them to see what other parents are doing, what the March for Our Lives students are doing, what responders to 9/11 have done and continue to do. I want them to see the work of gun safety advocates, and now, I want them to see what first responders during the coronavirus pandemic are doing. The list goes on.

We cannot get trapped by moments and by what *happened* to us. Ultimately, we have to find ways to move forward from tragic moments, as well as from ecstatic and joyful moments in life. In the end, what shapes your future is how you respond to your moments. In fact, it is in the aftermath of some of this country's worst times that American heroes and leaders have emerged.

Most Americans—and most people in the world—want nothing more than a safe family environment, a good education for their kids, and stability in the world. I hope my message can be the calm against chaos, the light against darkness. I've decided to be a helper, and I won't stop fighting until the world is better. Two years in, I'm only now getting started.

Chapter 1

A Family's Shock and Awe

The collapse of the World Trade Center on 9/11

On 9/11, I was already living in South Florida and working for Johnson & Johnson as a territory manager throughout most of the state. I kissed my wife, Jen, and my ten-month-old son, Jesse, goodbye before flying down to the Florida Keys to visit with our customers.

I landed and, as I always do, I pulled out my phone to call my wife to check in.

Jen asked me, "Have you heard what's happening?"

"No," I said.

She said, "A plane flew into the World Trade Center!"

A colleague I was traveling with and I watched the unfolding events on an airport TV. My eyes glued to the screen, we watched as the second tower was hit. We stood there in complete shock.

In a daze, we checked out our rental car to attend our first call with a mental health center.

Knowing my brother, Michael, I was certain he would be on the scene at the World Trade Center. As Deputy Medical Director of the New York City Fire Department (FDNY), his office was close by. I couldn't focus on work. We finished the visit, and then I persuaded my colleague to get in the car with me and start driving home.

"Something happened today that has turned the world upside down. Today is no longer about work, today is to focus on being Americans," I said.

It was clear to everyone that these events were not accidental. The twin towers had been hit, the Pentagon was hit, and a plane had crashed in Shanksville, Pennsylvania. We drove four hours to get back home. The whole way, family members were trying to connect with my brother Michael, a physician and first responder. Sadly, we kept getting the same updates: "Nothing." By the afternoon, we all assumed the worst.

By the later afternoon, my parents received a call from a stranger who was extremely calm. This wonderful woman had walked by the triage station that my brother and others had set up and said to all these first responders, including my brother, "I am sure you have loved ones. Give me a name and a phone number and I will call them."

Michael gave her the information. She didn't say anything else to him. She just called my parents. That was the sign of life that we desperately needed. She said, "Your relative is alive."

Apparently, this woman had made her way around this highly toxic and dangerous site, collecting phone numbers and calling loved ones. She gave them positive news they wouldn't otherwise have had on that day of destruction.

That woman, who refused to give her name, was a helper to our family and many other families, and she is one of the heroes of 9/11. Because of what happened to my family on September 11, 2001, and Valentine's Day, 2018, I have come to find greatness in people who do unexpectedly generous things in the moment—people who never intended to become heroes.

Sometime after midnight, Michael got through to all of us briefly. I'm sure he needed to connect with us, his family, even if just by phone, in the midst of such carnage. I can only imagine what he actually saw—and smelled. The scene has been described as a living hell.

Michael was a giant in the world of emergency services. As his career progressed, he became a premier speaker and leader; however, if called on to do so, he would have returned to the scene of 9/11. That is who he was.

Like other first responders, my brother was always the person running into danger while others were running from it. That was true on 9/11. After the first plane struck, my brother and other doctors headed to the World Trade Center site to set up their triage station.

He'd just come into the office that morning and was waiting for breakfast when the assignment to head for the World

Trade Center came in on his pager. "I don't recall the exact street, but we went over the Brooklyn Bridge, and as we were about one block away from the assigned location, there was an [extraordinarily] loud explosion. There were people starting to evacuate from the area, and then we noticed the tower that was burning—and as we were one block away from the assignment, we heard [another] extraordinarily loud explosion, and with that, many more people went running in the opposite direction, at which point I guess there was a few seconds of radio silence, and then somebody came over the air and said, 'A second plane just hit the other tower.'"[1]

Michael and his team were setting up triage at a loading dock when they started to hear a rumbling sound. "You know, there were rumors of additional planes missing, and actually, my initial thought was this was actually another plane… Just off to the right, there was a door with a fairly long, narrow hallway, and at this point, between police, and FBI, and EMS people, there were probably about twenty-plus people in this loading dock area. We all stuffed ourselves into this hallway and pulled the door shut, and then the noise just got very loud and the room filled with dust."

Michael thought he would die there, and he tried to call my parents to say goodbye. Thank God he didn't get through.

"The noise stopped," he remembered, "and we opened up the door, and everything was pitch-black. The way we got in [through] the loading dock was not the way we were getting out. It was obstructed."

---

[1] This section with Michael's account is excerpted from an interview he gave for the World Trade Center Task Force Review on October 2, 2001.

They found their way out, though, through another door. And he ran. "I wasn't close enough to anybody with a radio in hand. It was frustrating as hell, I can tell you, when the cell sites went down, which was right—really as soon as this incident began. All I wanted to do after I got out and a safe distance away was actually just call my folks and say, you know, 'I'm alive,' and that was the worst thing. I mean, it took hours and hours for the cell sites to come back up, at least at Sprint. That was really for me the worst part of this whole thing, was not being able to make a phone call."

"In a bizarre way, the best person on the street there that day was some little old Spanish lady who says, 'I live a couple of blocks from here.' She had a pad and a pen, took down a list of names, a list of phone numbers—took down a list of names and phone numbers and called, and she got ahold of my parents about two hours before I did."

When the noise stopped, and the shaking stopped, the door they'd used to enter the building was blocked, but they found another door out. Rather than getting the hell out of there, covered in dust as they were, my brother and his group returned to the command post to resume setting up. This team spent sixteen days at Ground Zero treating people. But only years later would the pieces of what really transpired during those weeks come together.

Surprised to find themselves still alive, the men and women who were on the scene began what could be described as "the long climb to recovery." Crawling out from under vehicles after what seemed like an hour of entrapment in a suffocating environment and wading through mountains of debris, they entered a new reality—a post-9/11 world: a world of darkness, choking air, and "deafening silence."

While my family and I were receiving phone calls from various parts of the country (pre-internet!), frantically exchanging possibilities around what could have happened to Michael—and making assumptions based on what we knew of him as a typical first responder focused on helping others—we feared the worst. The chances of survival, let alone saving others, left us very pessimistic.

The primary emergency medical services (EMS) provider for New York City is the FDNY EMS Division. In addition, more than thirty hospital systems (referred to as "voluntaries") contract with the city to provide 911 response units, delivering full-time, professional service to specific areas of the city. In 2001, there were approximately 950 ambulance tours every day for a city of more than eight million residents and countless tourists. Assuming each unit had a minimum two-member crew on board, nearly 200 EMTs and paramedics were on site when the towers fell. By evening, an estimated 400 additional EMS personnel had made their way to the World Trade Center.

First responders like my brother were driven by what had always motivated them—helping people. My brother never thought about his own safety and well-being when it was time to help others. A couple of months after 9/11, there was a plane crash in Rockaway, New York. At first, nobody knew if it was an act of terrorism or not. My brother was, again, one of the first on the scene. For most, like me, our drive is to stay away from danger. Thankfully, our first responders are wired differently, and they run toward it. Why? To help us. My brother never thought about this as heroic. He considered this his obligation. In fact, he never wanted his legacy to be about these moments in his life. He wanted his legacy to be about all of the other first responders that he helped to train and mentor. My son, currently nineteen years old, is now one of them. It scares my wife and me to no end, but he is wired like my brother. He is more concerned with the safety of others than he is with his own.

Chapter 2

Portrait of a Hero

My brother Michael

Almost every moment related to my brother's life that I can think of had to do with his dream of being a doctor and being the first on the scene to lend a helping hand to someone—literally always. Throughout the years, he pushed for a strong health care system for everyone, a better way to do things, and relentless support for anyone he came in contact with who needed a mentor.

One of his best friends, Maria Artuso, was the emergency room nursing director when Michael became the ER medical director at LIJ Forest Hills Medical Center in 2009. "He wanted the best possible care for his patients, and he wouldn't stop until he got it. He developed protocols and policies to make the patient experience better when they came through his emergency room. Every time you spoke to him, he was going to a [work] dinner or a lecture, or working on some project. You never heard him say he was going to swim, or the beach. For him, it was always about work and revolved around emergency medicine!"

Michael's interest in living the life of a first responder started early. As a teenager, my brother rode his bicycle to volunteer with the Commack Volunteer Ambulance Corps on Long Island. Later in life, he went to medical school, and then returned to the Tri-State area to work in emergency medicine. His hard work eventually led him to become the medical director for the Emergency Services department at Northwell Health in New York.

John D'Angelo, senior vice president and executive director of Emergency Medicine Services, saw professional stardom in Michael as soon as they shook hands. Prior to John becoming his boss, they were colleagues in the same roles at two different community hospitals; then, a change in the organization meant that Michael now reported to John.

"I've always known him to be a guy who [has] high energy, always worked hard, [and] dealt with capacity issues in a small facility because two or three other hospitals had closed the prior year," John recalls. "He had position shortages and filled in the gap. Once I became [the person] in charge, it was apparent not only was he extremely hard working and tireless, but I don't think I've worked with anyone more dedicated to his patients—not just the job—and the people that worked for him."

Michael would often call John on a Sunday afternoon and get excited about certain things that were happening relating to work, and John would have to urge him to keep his "day off" as a day off! According to John, Michael mentored numerous people and had a real following that included both young and old people. His heart for paramedics/EMTs led him to crisis situations in Westchester, New York City, and Long Island. He sat on county committees and national chapters in emergency medicine and directly created policies.

When Northwell became more active within its larger care system in providing the medical oversight for a growing ambulance corps, Michael saw a real need to improve an existing fellowship program with residents in it, and physicians who were medical directors. It wasn't being run as well as it could be, so Northwell made Mike the medical director of the EMS operation. He really took that energy and advanced their care models and deliveries. He fearlessly pushed the envelope at the county and state levels and was very innovative and forward-thinking.

John added, "He led by example. Clinically, he wasn't just someone who would just create policies or do lectures and tell people what they should do. He was out there *doing* them. He worked clinically more than any director I had. People followed him because he always had their backs and worked just as hard as anybody else. Sometimes there is a bad outcome in medicine. If there was a question of whether care could have been better, Michael would want to know if that person was okay first. And he was really bright. He brought medical knowledge, he was well respected by all the other chairs and physicians because he was extremely [intelligent] and knew his stuff. Even when people didn't agree on processes, he would always bring the conversation back to what was best for the patient."

Michael helped to establish the Second Chance brunch or luncheon, where Northwell brings in people who've experienced cardiac arrest to meet their rescuers during EMS Week. They sit at a table and tell the story of what it means to have a second chance, and in turn, the rescuers describe the significance of helping them. Michael also started that in the fire department, with at least a dozen survivors benefitting each year. Always a proponent of education, Michael also helped to establish a scholarship for paramedics aspiring to go to medical school.

"He pushed me!" Maria insisted. "He pushed many people to expand their careers. I was contemplating what to do my master's degree in and he completely pushed me to be a nurse practitioner so I could have that autonomy. He did this with many other nurses and leaders. Michael showed us the right way to take care of patients."

Sal Pardo, director of the Emergency Department at Long Island Jewish Medical Center, crossed paths with my brother and never left. They would play golf at the Sagamore Resort in Lake George and then participate in the medical conference afterwards, but that's not what he chuckles about. Sal experienced other moments with Michael outside of their shared profession in the paradigm of corporate health care at Northwell. They became close confidantes.

Michael was very much into the everyday rituals of life's routine, and that would show up in many ways. He would purchase two ice teas from Dunkin' Donuts every day, so he would always have one in one hand to drink and one in the other hand, waiting. It became a running joke. He was very regimented: *same day, same way.*

He's been there in the challenging times of my life, through my divorce, and becoming a single parent to a young son. I was basically asked to leave my house, and out of respect for my ex-wife, I left. I went to my sister's, but she was unable to accommodate me. She was going through her own thing. Mike opened his house to me, saying, "I'm no fun to live with!"…I soon realized that he was not kidding. I am not the neatest person around, and Michael had to have neatness and orderliness."

Michael had a large network of friends, including a group of people who were with him on 9/11 and were now all coming down with uniquely strange and extreme symptoms. The correlation was clear to those in the group. When he first developed severe itching, Michael confided in our sister, Abbie, who was also a physician. He had recently been on a trip to the Caribbean, and she suggested that he may have gotten hepatitis; as a result, he ran his own blood tests at work and found that his liver enzymes were elevated. He then had a variety of medical tests in early July, 2013. A few weeks went by with all the results being normal. Then his symptoms progressed, and his urine changed color.

Even though Michael was a doctor, our sister was a doctor, and he was surrounded by doctors urging him to take additional tests, he put it off as long as he could get away with it. I think he invented the clichéd notion *too busy to be sick.* That was his mindset.

Finally, toward the end of 2013, he had an MRI. Sal was with him when he received the report, which said: "Suspicious mass in the pancreatic head."

Sal said, "I hope you're taking this seriously." Sal knew my brother well. He knew he had to convince him to pursue validation, a true diagnosis. At this point, Abbie and Sal were the only ones who knew as Michael began his journey toward what would become a pancreatic cancer diagnosis.

"He still was not ready to deal with being sick," said Sal. "He said it could be an over-read by a radiologist." But after getting a biopsy, the pathology report unfortunately confirmed the condition that would become Michael's death sentence.

The way my brother handled his cancer was consistent with who he was. Michael spent the next years teaching, in addition to working. Medical students and residents at all the major hospitals in New York, likely learned emergency management through classes with Michael or were mentored by him.

Following his diagnosis, one evening, Michael was teaching a class in which he presented a set of symptoms. He worked with the class to put together a treatment plan. At the end of the class, Michael informed the students that *he* was the patient. Immediately following the class, he went to the hospital and started to unfold this plan of attack to deal with his cancer. He already knew where this was headed, being a doctor, but he transformed *his own illness* into a teaching situation.

Three weeks later at Columbia University Hospital, while waiting for a surgical procedure to remove the cancerous mass from his pancreas, with me, my parents, and our brother Ira by his side, Michael was approached by a resident who was going to be on the surgical team operating on him, who said, "Dr. Guttenberg, you probably don't remember me, but I know you."

My brother said, "I apologize. How did we meet?"

The man said, "Three weeks ago, you taught a class and I was in it. You presented a series of symptoms and then you told us that you were the patient. Now, you are my patient. Every resident in this hospital knows you are here, and we are going to make sure you are taken care of."

Michael was about to undergo a Whipple procedure, also known as a *pancreaticoduodenectomy*, a complex operation to remove the head of the pancreas, the first part of the small intestine (or duodenum), the gallbladder, and the bile duct. The Whipple procedure is used to treat tumors and other disorders of the pancreas, intestine, and bile duct. It is the most frequently used surgery to treat pancreatic cancer confined to the head of the pancreas. After performing the Whipple procedure, your surgeon reconnects the remaining organs to allow you to digest food normally after surgery.

The Whipple procedure is a difficult and demanding operation that can have serious risks. However, this surgery can sometimes be lifesaving, particularly for people with early-stage pancreatic cancer.

For Michael, the procedure became complicated and took between eight and nine hours; however, the mass was removed.

According to John D'Angelo, although Michael had expressed anxiety as a result of the diagnosis and would be required to undergo medical and intense chemotherapy after surgery, work did not stop.

"I can't tell you how often I was on the phone with him," John explained. "He was a little stir-crazy. He wanted to do what he loved. I would get calls from HR in the hospital that he was [working] in the emergency department when he shouldn't have been there due to his [undergoing] chemo and [the] potential for infection. He just had a real hard time not being active. He was on partial disability, and we had to make sure he wasn't in a patient facility while he was getting care, so we gave him an office for whenever he wanted to come in and do busywork like policies and manuals."

My brother was tackling pancreatic cancer—which is largely incurable, and hanging on, facing down an ominous one-year survival rate of 20 percent—and he was still focused on creating policies and manuals!

Eventually, in 2013, Michael took a position at another hospital as the chair of the emergency department. He was the type of guy who was unfazed by the condition of the hospital he was going to run, something that others may be wary about. This particular hospital wasn't well known as a highly functioning or easy place to work, but he thrived when he took on seemingly impossible tasks and stepped into roles where he could make a difference.

Michael's lifelong tenacity and his commitment to others over and above his own safety seemed a little crazy to me, but soon, I would come to learn about the blind passion and determination it takes to fulfill a mission.

Chapter 3

Genes of Humanity

My fiftieth birthday with Michael

After my sister, Abbie, was born, my parents went through two miscarriages. They consulted a specialist who informed them that pregnancy was no longer possible.

Due to these circumstances, my older brother, Ira, is adopted. For years, my parents had understood they could no longer have children, so they never worried about protection.

Then one day, my dad came home from work to find my mom beaming. "Guess what?" She told him she was pregnant. That was with me! They thought it was a fluke. It was not.

Whatever the problem was, it had corrected itself. And thirteen months after I was born, Michael came along. Two years later, my brother, Paul, came into the world. Then Mom had her tubes tied! I was now one of five kids, four boys, and one girl, growing up in a house on Long Island. Abbie was the only one who scored her own room.

As the oldest of the siblings and tough as nails, Abbie looked after us, taking on a maternal role. (She takes care of her "little brothers" to this day.) Abbie exercised control over us boys. To deal with our acting out, she made up a secret agency called the BBB, the "Bad Boy Bureau." All she had to do was inform us that she was going to call them, and we would behave.

I really don't blame Abbie for this clever approach to babysitting and for keeping her little brothers in line. But at least it wasn't because our parents were overtly neglectful. In fact, they're pretty special people and integral to my story of two American tragedies.

Our mom was a registered nurse and worked the overnight shift so she could be with us when we got home from school. When I was in middle school back in the 1970s, evidence of the women's movement was not yet visible to me. Still, my mom abhorred doctors calling her "girl" and talking down to her, so she went back to school and earned her master's degree in health care administration. She ended up getting a job doing utilization review for an insurance company. In her new role, *she* could tell *doctors* what they could or could not do, overseeing decisions by those same people who had degraded her. When my mother took on that assignment, she found her voice, and she never shut up!

Her experiences in the workforce awakened her politically. She became very active in the National Organization for Women (NOW) and ran for state representative in New York in the early eighties. She ran twice, both times against a person whose name was in itself a brand, or even an institution. She did not win, but we could not have been prouder of my mom.

My mom is a fighter.

Two parents who always did the right thing raised me; they did everything with strength and compassion. Their kids were the beneficiaries of this show of upstanding character.

My dad owned a pharmacy that was intentionally about forty-five minutes away from our home. Dad loved his customers, but he also wanted to be able to come home and focus on just his family. The only way to do that was maintain physical distance between his business and his home. The man never missed a day of work except for the day after his knee surgery, which, back then, was a big surgery. He made it home every day, rain or snow. One day, his car got turned around on the highway in snowy weather; the car was pointed backwards for a while until he managed to turn it around again. Thankfully, he was the only one on the highway that night! He believed more than ever that the pharmacy needed to be open that day for his customers.

My dad's grit, determination, and unbelievable work ethic still complement my mother's spirit and keen intelligence, even now that they're in their eighties.

I have always been close to my dad. I have long admired his entrepreneurship. I also love the way his mind works. As a kid, I used to love listening to my dad. I watched him challenge people to do what was right. Because he was so clear, concise, and forceful, I grew up wanting to emulate him. My respect for my dad and our true friendship led me to ask him to be the best man at my wedding. He was the obvious choice.

I am very fortunate that my parents set the example for us that they did. Their qualities shine through me and my siblings. We grew up to be strong, independent people who are decent and fight for what's right in our country.

Chapter 4

Grounds for Activism

Exiting Michael's funeral

While with the Fire Department of New York (FDNY) on an EMS fellowship, Michael responded to the World Trade Center terror attacks on September 11, 2001, and worked "on the pile"—the post-9/11 wreckage of the World Trade Center. As we now know, the site's dust and smoke were laden with dangerous organic material and countless toxicants such as jet fuel, PCBs, and dioxins as well as pulverized glass, drywall, and cement.

The Journal of Emergency Medical Services would report years later, "The lasting effect of 9/11 is the physical and emotional toll that continues to plague those who responded. New York City's officials estimate that more than 21,000 people who worked either on a paid or volunteer basis after 9/11 have developed physical and mental disorders as a result of their exposure to toxic substances and traumatic experiences…. For many, the effects cost them their livelihoods and/or relationships."

Since 9/11, many serious health issues, including chronic respiratory infections and gastrointestinal diseases, have been directly correlated to the acrid dust and smoke breathed in by those on scene. Testing completed by the EPA in the days following the collapse of the towers revealed a complexity of chemical compounds and particulate structures unlike anything ever encountered.

Dust particles, especially those in the air immediately following the collapse of the buildings, were measured at ten microns or less—particles so small that they are capable of doing damage regardless of their chemical content because of their ability to be inhaled and transferred deep into the lower lungs.

For years, first responders fought for health benefits to help pay for the expensive tests and treatments they required. Gradually, as studies acknowledged that the health issues were due to exposure to toxins as a result of the 9/11 attack, responders began to receive healthcare coverage, but how much and when varied widely.

On January 2, 2010, President Barack Obama signed the James Zadroga 9/11 Health and Compensation Act, establishing the World Trade Center Health Program and providing $4.3 billion in federal funding for both treatment and financial compensation to those suffering effects of the attacks. This action helped, but because of the slow-moving wheels of bureaucracy, it came very late for responders who had already endured years of fiscal, physical, and emotional hardship. Some had already died.

Once Michael was diagnosed, he recovered quickly from the surgery. It was pretty remarkable. As a workaholic, he had every intention of returning to work as soon as possible, and he pushed himself to do that. He was living in Tarrytown, an hour outside of Manhattan, and his townhouse was four stories high with lots of steps. My parents insisted on being there with him, but the steps were a challenge for them. He had good friends who helped while he underwent chemo and radiation treatments. My sister, brothers, and I traveled and did all that we could to help as often as possible. Eventually, he completed the treatment and flourished again. He looked terrific.

During that same period, Abbie's closest childhood friend, who lived on Long Island, was also sick with cancer. Between her and Michael, Abbie was in New York every two or three weeks. Abbie often went to Broadway shows and restaurants with Michael, in an effort to do things with him to distract him from anything having to do with his diagnosis.

For the most part, Michael felt well after the chemo and radiation. He carried on with his wonderful friends and great career at Northwell Hospital as their director of emergency medical services. His illness, however, returned with a vengeance in 2016, as spots in his lungs. Eventually, it hit his stomach and his liver and shut down his digestive system. He loved food more than anything and enjoyed going out to dinner with friends. But because of the effect of the cancer on his gastrointestinal system, he was robbed of so many mealtime conversations while breaking bread with family and friends…countless joyous moments lost.

I sold the final pieces of my Dunkin' Donuts business in November 2016, when he was pretty sick. This provided me with the flexibility and opportunity to devote more time to his care, rather than just hanging out with him when I could squeeze in the time. It also gave me the opportunity to help him prepare for his death, his funeral, and settling his estate. My sister was his medical proxy, and I handled his personal affairs.

My brother and I were only thirteen months apart and had always shared many of the same friends; we had a unique closeness because of this. I suspect that closeness, together with my business background, is the reason he asked me to handle his business and personal affairs. My sister, who never stopped taking care of her little brothers, was a physician and was therefore a natural to fill the role of his medical proxy. We were fortunate to have a lot of siblings, and we were always there for one another. But our family had never gone through anything like this before. We were dealing with the idea of illness and loss for the first time. My brother, who was always there for others, did not want to have to prepare for the end of life by himself. He now needed the help of others. For me, being there to help my brother in his final years started me on a process of purpose, one that went beyond the immediate circle of my wife and children.

After the initial shock and sadness of his diagnosis, the focus turned to managing the treatment. Because Michael had rarely traveled out of the country, Abbie made a point of taking him to see Jordan, where her son, Ryan, was studying Arabic, and then to Israel to visit her exchange student's family. That trip stimulated Michael beyond his wildest dreams, but it also reminded him that the odds of his doing it again would be next to impossible.

His last year of life became one horrendous nightmare. All that he had breathed in at what is now Ground Zero charged through his cells, simply ravaging him. Michael Guttenberg was a *victim*, though he hated that term.

Ironically, the last photos snapped of our whole family, including both my brother and my daughter, were taken when we were visiting the 9/11 memorial during a private tour in August of

2017. I connected with the 9/11 memorial because I was on this mission to do more to recognize the first responders who didn't die that day. Back in 2015, I started trying to find and speak with a decision-maker involved with the memorial. After using every networking connection I had, I was connected with the senior vice president of the memorial who manages community affairs. I shared my ideas for wanting to honor those first responders and workers who survived. Eventually, a process was put in place that led to an addition to the 9/11 memorial known as "The Glade." While I was very humbled to have played a small role in that, my brother never wanted me to pursue this kind of thing and never wanted me to do it for him. Michael did not want the story of his life to be just about 9/11. It was a source of disagreement between us, and he would get upset with me for making such a fuss. For me, it defined his adult life. My hope now is when people visit the 9/11 memorial, that they will go to The Glade to reflect on all of the amazing heroes who survived and who worked to make a difference on that day and who have had to struggle through years of illness since.

I told him, "You did this, and you are a hero. I know you're humble, but this country needs to understand what you and others like you have done." He was unable to see himself as a hero and did not consider what he did to be "exceptional." It was his job, and he would have done it again if he'd had the chance. Michael was clear about what he saw as his legacy. He wanted the story of his life to be his work as a first responder and his teaching and mentoring of other first responders. Seeing the success of EMS providers, physicians, nurses, and others he'd taught or mentored was his source of pride. Sadly, Michael is now missing the greatest part of his legacy. Following his death, our youngest brother, Paul, at the age of forty-nine, joined the Commack

Volunteer Ambulance Corps—the same place where Michael began his emergency service career as a teen volunteer.

Even closer to home, my son Jesse, who idolized his Uncle Michael, plans on studying to become an EMT and firefighter and to make this his life career. Jesse donated some of his bar mitzvah money to honor his Uncle Michael and all first responders, funding a plaque at the entrance of the Commack Volunteer Ambulance Corps building.

Michael knew time was running short. I tried to encourage him, saying, "You're not a normal human being. You're more like a cat with nine lives. You survived the World Trade Center and a diagnosis of pancreatic cancer. You still have lives left. Don't lose hope yet."

He said, "Don't forget, I've been shot at twice!" It was not an exaggeration. Early in his career, he rode ambulances as an EMT through Jamaica, Queens, a tough area at the time. During this period, he was shot at twice, though never hit.

"Exactly," I said. "You're not ready to leave this earth yet." He was a hero and a fighter, the definition of *tough*.

I constantly urged Michael to find a financial planner to do estate planning. I urge everyone I meet now to complete their estate planning when they're healthy. It is a different experience when you are sick and know that you will be dying. You go through this knowing that you are planning for your death. Michael had always put it off, but shortly before he died, he finally decided that he was ready. On Tuesday, September 19, 2017, I was about to leave on my flight to New York. Michael and I finally committed to working together on his financial and estate planning and decided we would spend that week on it. We would meet with a financial planner, accountant, and attorney. I called him that morning before boarding the plane, and he was not doing well.

I said, "Go to one of your hospitals, get checked out, and I will be there."

He snapped, "If you're going to bust my chops and give me a hard time, don't come!" His attitude indicated that his helplessness was setting in. He had snapped for good reason.

By the time I got there, he was in the hospital and never left. Because of all the chemo, his bone marrow stopped working, and he developed a septic infection that he could not fight. He was on a feeding tube because his stomach no longer worked. He could no longer undergo chemo. This meant that my brother's time was coming to an end. We were thirteen months apart, and I was staring down his death at the age of fifty, which forced me to think of my own life with a new sense of urgency.

Knowing that he was out of options, Michael decided the time had come to stop the feeding tube. As a family, we tried to encourage him to remain on it, but he knew he would never get out of the hospital. We chose not to make that decision for him. His mind was still sharp as a tack, and he had simply had enough.

In his mind, he had nothing to live for any longer. Two days later, he was transported to hospice. I'll never forget leaving that hospital. My brother was a giant in the world of emergency service and his colleagues were there with multiple vehicles and in full dress, waiting for Michael at the entrance to transport him. Our family was thinking we would transport him ourselves and had no idea his colleagues had prepared to do this.

The memory of this drive is etched in my head; it was just so surreal. It was a beautiful and sunny day with not a cloud in the sky. Pulling out of the hospital and onto the exit for the highway, multiple ambulances and emergency vehicles surrounded us, taking this final ride along with our family and my brother to his home so that he could walk through it one final time, and then to the hospice, knowing that his life was ending. My sister rode along in the ambulance with my brother. When I asked her what the drive was like in the ambulance, she said it was "Just very quiet."

The reality of what was happening was settling in. My brother was emotional due to the significance of the moment. Our family, also overwhelmed with feeling, was in awe of those showing up to support Michael. We knew that people would come to his funeral. However, witnessing his colleagues showing up to escort him from the hospital to the hospice was powerful. These amazing men and women were there to let my brother know how much he meant to them. I often think of unexpected moments like this when helpers come out to lift us up at a time when we need it the most.

My brother was in hospice for over a month. Enabling Michael's iced tea addiction, our brother Paul would drop one off every day. Michael's heart and brain were still strong, so when he decided to stop nutrition, his body's final end took longer than normal. Michael's friend Sal called me the "guardian of the door," because even though he was anxious for things to be over, my brother allowed friends to visit whenever they wanted, which isn't the normal experience at hospice. His friends were supportive and kept showing up to spend all the time they could with him. As a result, Michael would end up completely exhausted, so I began to limit the coming and goings—something he would not have done himself. One day, after a few weeks, Michael told Sal, "I thought this would be a lot quicker." He would always say he wasn't in pain.

A few days before he died, Michael requested a family dinner. We set up a table with a mound of Italian food in his hospice room and attempted to give Michael the type of spirited family dinner we'd always had, though our hearts were shattering. My parents and siblings will never forget that dinner, as it was also the last time we were able to get Michael out of bed. He slept for most of his remaining days.

My parents, my siblings, and I were with Michael for almost the entire time he was in hospice. It was the most time that we had spent together as adults, and sadly, it was to say goodbye. What made it easier were the amazing people at hospice, who did everything that they could to accommodate us and to make us feel at home. More importantly, they attended to his every need, making his final weeks, days, and moments pain-free. I will be forever grateful to the great people at hospice who were helpers to our family, just as they are to so many other families in need.

Chapter 5

Legacy in Lights

Michael's funeral

The day that we visited the 9/11 memorial as a family, Michael had one very specific request for his family.

"I have never asked for anything or any recognition," he told us. "Now, I have only one wish. At my funeral, I want a lot of ambulances, fire trucks, and police cars, and I want to shut down the fucking roads." What Michael said was true. He had never asked for any recognition. In the end, he wanted to be honored in a way that he would never have asked for at any previous time in his life. I don't know why this came up for him at the end—I'd be guessing if I tried to analyze it. We recognized the significance of the request as soon as he asked, and all we needed to say about it was "Done." There was no need for more discussion about the whys.

Making sure that Michael had the funeral that he wanted and deserved became my mission. When Michael went into the hospice, my sister and I went to work planning. I called a few of his closest friends from work, and they connected me with the New York City Fire Department. We were informed that he would be buried with full honors. They coordinated with agencies across New York to ensure that Michael's wishes would be met and that he would be appropriately honored.

Michael's funeral on Long Island and burial in Queens did just that. It was kicked off a few days earlier at the hospice facility, when his staff and twenty vehicles from multiple emergency service agencies showed up to pay their final respects as his body was carried out of hospice.

On the day of his funeral, there were dozens of emergency vehicles, a helicopter flying overhead, and a large American flag hanging over the road heading out from the funeral home. Michael's wish had come true. As he requested, they "closed down the fucking roads," including the Southern State Parkway. If you're from New York, you know that's a big deal! Michael's funeral drew approximately five hundred people and a combined total of seventy-five ambulances, fire trucks, and police escorts. Michael received the honor that he deserved.

Michael's body was transported in a 1967 Cadillac ambulance belonging to the Commack Volunteer Ambulance Corps. As it was where his life in emergency service began at the age of fourteen, it was only appropriate that his journey would end with them at the age of fifty. Up until the day he died, he was on their board. It has never been lost on me that the ambulance was a 1967 Cadillac—the year that Michael was born.

Michael's influence lives on in so many. "I don't think he realized the impact he made on people," his friend Maria said of him. "There is not a day that goes by that Northwell Health is not recognizing him or doing something in his honor. Ambulances are dedicated to him with his name on it. I hope he sees that from above, because you don't see that often! He wanted me to start traveling because he never did. He wanted me to enjoy life, and always knew that every problem has a solution. And he was right."

We returned home from Michael's funeral just prior to my wife's birthday. I remember sitting down with her and the kids and saying with a big sigh, "After all we've been through, what do you want for your birthday?"

"You want the truth?" she replied. "Another dog!"

Given that we are a family of hardcore dog lovers, this request had come up before. We have our dog, Charli, an amazing white goldendoodle. Though I wasn't a fan of getting a second dog, how could I possibly say no after we had just dealt with my brother's death? Then the kids chimed in. I was powerless to prevent the acquisition. All three of them immediately ran to get on the internet and check out the breeder's site. Not long after that, we had our second goldendoodle, a beautiful black and grey puppy. This decision would turn out to be one of the greatest we ever made, as our collective life would soon encounter additional trauma. We really needed our dogs.

Following Michael's funeral, for the first time in my adult life, I had nothing to do (except take care of a puppy, of course). I had worked for Johnson & Johnson from 1991 through 2004, and then had my own business from 2004 through November of 2016. Then I was taking care of Michael. With his death, I had a lot of free time. Jen encouraged me to take the rest of the year to do nothing, to simply relax. Unfortunately, I am not good at waking up and "doing nothing." I am a person who needs a plan, who needs to be busy, who needs a purpose. But in the end, for a few months, outside of doing a little auto brokering and real estate, I did nothing.

By January, I was climbing the walls, desperate for a purpose. I started looking for opportunities. Every task up to this point had simply been about finding ways to keep busy just to get through the day, without anything involving working toward a goal or a mission.

But sometimes, driving purpose falls into our lives as the result of painful moments, moments that can also serve as a catalyst for something greater.

What happened on 9/11 was a defining part of my family's life story. Soon, though, it would become secondary to another unexpected and pivotal moment.

Chapter 6

Hunted on a Day of Love

My baby girl

There is never a dull moment when you're the father of two teenagers. The morning of February 14 was no different. My two kids, who loved each other very much but also acted up around each other like any other siblings, were running late and getting angry at one another for it. My dogs were barking and needing attention, and my wife and I needed to leave. I was so busy rushing them out the door that morning, repeatedly insisting, "You have to get to school," that I do not think I said, "I love you." Never in a million years did I believe at the time that I would be rushing them into a school shooting and that this would be the last moment with my daughter—and my last words to her. Knowing what I know now, I always tell everyone to make sure that they look their loved ones in the eye every chance that they get and say "I love you" as if they will not get the chance to say it again. I learned the hard way that this scenario is reality for far too many American families.

Jesse watched over Jaime like a hawk. He always made sure she was okay and safe and that no one was messing with her. In fact, he experienced anxiety about the safety and security of his family. Normally, parents call to check on their kids. However, Jesse, who worried about our well-being and security, was always checking in on *us*. Maybe this was the future first responder in him, or maybe he just needed to know we were okay.

So when Jesse called me on February 14 just after 2:00 p.m., at first, I assumed our regular routine was playing out. As Jesse could be a bit of a jokester, it was not always clear when to take him seriously. He would often start off by saying, "Dad!" and I'd reply, "What?" Then he'd launch into an elaborate story. Jesse and I both share a passion for cars, and usually his calls had something to do with a car that he'd seen and the reasons why we needed to have that car.

"Dad!" Jesse shouted into the phone.

"Yes, Jesse?"

"There is a shooter at my school!" he screamed.

Not yet sure if I should take him seriously, I responded, "What are you talking about?"

"And I can't find Jaime!" Jesse's voice cracked.

Once he mentioned Jaime, I knew this was real. My son would never joke about his sister's safety. My breath caught in my throat. "Where are you?"

"I'm running," he said, and then repeated, "I can't find Jaime." I told him to keep running as fast as he could, but he could not stop worrying about Jaime. As I stayed on the phone with Jesse, he suddenly shouted, "I'm hearing bullets!" The bullets he heard then were the ones from the third floor that were killing his sister and others inside.

I said, "You run! Run faster and get out of there." But rather than listening to me, he just kept saying, "But I can't find Jaime." His fear for his sister's life paralyzed him.

Jesse ran and ran because he knew he had no choice. He ran for his life. Jen and I convinced him that we would handle worrying about Jaime. Otherwise, he would have gone back into Marjory Stoneman Douglas High School (MSD), gunfire or not, to search for his fourteen-year-old sister, whose class was on the third floor.

Minutes later, my wife, a pediatric occupational therapist, ended up on lockdown at the school where she was working, which was around the corner from MSD. I told her I was going to find Jesse and figure out a way to reach Jaime. If I had to go through people's front lawns, fire trucks, and red emergency tape, I didn't care. I would get there. Jesse ended up at a nearby Walmart, and that's where I met him. It turned out that while Jesse was there, the killer had also fled to the store, camouflaging himself among the fleeing students.

I arrived at the Walmart and got as close to the building as I could. I picked up Jesse, who quickly jumped in the car with me and accessed the "Find my iPhone" function from his phone to locate Jaime's phone. We knew it was still in the building, but we were hoping she had dropped it. She wasn't trying to reach us via text or phone call like the other kids were doing. We kept trying to call and text her, praying someone would pick up the phone and give it back to her.

We started calling Jaime's friends' parents, with our fear and panic intensifying. My wife and I both posted on Facebook, asking anyone with information to call us. Law enforcement instructed parents who couldn't reach their kids to go to a Marriott Hotel where busses would be dropping kids off.

Several friends of ours went to the Marriott to wait. We knew that if she could have reached us, she would have. If she was with someone else, she would have used their phone. Jaime was the kind of kid who communicated *everything* to her mother. If her shoelace became untied, she would have texted Jen to let her know. When we did not hear from her, we knew something was wrong. We decided to go to the hospital, hoping that she was there being tended to and not worse off.

The thing about a mass shooting in your own neighborhood is that in real-time, there is no time for thought or planning. You can't determine if your actions are helpful or a hindrance. Should we have gone to the hospital ourselves or waited with the rest of the community? Waiting at home with panic setting in was not an option.

When we arrived at the hospital, we saw other families who also had not yet been able to locate loved ones. After waiting for over an hour, we were told that neither this hospital nor any other local hospital had any record of Jaime.

My sister, Abbie, even reached out to other ER doctors from her hospital in Cincinnati. Michael had friends who worked in emergency medicine in Florida, and she contacted them with Jaime's description. The thought of her having been caught up in a mass shooting was unfathomable. Abbie called Michael's former boss, Dr. John D'Angelo, to track down ER doctors in Florida, hoping somebody had information or had seen her.

I am fortunate to have many friends in law enforcement. One of my best friends, Lieutenant Scott Myers with the Coral Springs Police Department, was about to see the bloodshed at my children's high school with his own eyes. I knew Scott because our daughters were involved in dance together. He and I were fellow "dance dads," fathers who became friends through our daughters. As the young women danced and became more competitive, the dads spent more time together building their dance competition props and traveling on excursions. Our wives became close, too.

Scott was in his office when the call went out for first responders. "Along with everyone else in my department, we furiously made our way up to the high school. It was literally our whole department. People were flowing out of the building like it was on fire. It wasn't one or two people, it was everybody. The shooting was still in progress, which reinforced the urgency in trying to resolve the issue and stop the bleeding, literally.

"When I arrived on the scene, it was still going on, or at least that is what I was being told by my dispatcher. When I got there, in my mind, I didn't feel I had time to open up my trunk and get out my rifle. I felt like every second mattered, and I ended up running into the building with two other guys and only my handgun. That was how urgent I felt the situation was. I knew it would be better to bring my rifle, but we could not wait. While it would give me more capabilities, I decided that every second mattered and to go in without it.

"As I was approaching the 1200 building, that is when I first saw one of the coaches deceased outside the building. That was when it became real for me. I guess in the back of my mind, I had been hoping this had been a false alarm or some sort of miscommunication. It sounded like it was the real deal, but you're hoping in a horrific event that it isn't genuine. But when we saw the coach down, we knew it was real. Then it just got more difficult from that moment on.

"We made our way into the building and we encountered the athletic director. He was still alive, but he had injuries that ultimately took his life. I had hoped he would survive because we were able to get him out of the building to the paramedics and first responders that were there. I didn't know he'd died. He was still alive when we passed him off to the next group of officers. My objective and goal was to kill the bad guy. It took a significant amount of time to confirm he had already exited the building. At that point, once we realized he was out of the building and no longer a threat, it became just a search and recovery operation. We started recovering and providing first aid. We got new information that the shooter was in a residential neighborhood not too far away. I took a couple of SWAT officers with me with the goal of apprehending him. As I arrived, he was being taken into custody. I was the highest-ranking officer on the scene, so I took control and he was taken into custody."

This was the first chance Scott had to call his wife, who let him know that Jen and I hadn't been able to find Jaime. "I almost dismissed it," Scott said, "because I figured either she was among the hundreds evacuated or she was hiding somewhere on campus. My original feeling was, *I'm sure she's okay and we just haven't heard from her*. I kind of reassured my wife. My mind was still focused on the event and that a criminal investigation needed to take place—a slew of professional issues I was going to have to deal with at this point."

I called Scott myself, and as he gave possibilities as to why Jaime might not have called, it was becoming apparent she would have been able to contact us. Sometime while Scott was on his way back to the high school, he learned the school had been evacuated. Secondary checks had been made, and no one was hiding. If they couldn't find Jaime, Scott knew that probably meant she was still on campus but not alive.

Scott's hopes started to diminish. He called his wife and told her to be prepared for the worst. "When I got back to the school," he said, "the FBI and sheriff's office were in charge. I told my boss that I needed to go back in and try to find her, that she was a friend of the family's, that I needed to positively identify her if she was still there. We made our way back in, and ultimately the medical examiner gave me approval to try and find her, which was helpful because the investigators didn't want to potentially contaminate the scene… They asked what she looked like. When I described her, they all put their heads down and recognized the fact that she was outside the school, just outside the building."

Scott had seen a lot of horrible things before: dead adults and dead kids—lots of horrible things. But that day, he identified my baby girl.

Right about that moment, I called him. Jen and I were in different cars, driving home from the hospital about twenty minutes away. I was driving directly behind her. We were working our way onto the highway.

"Any news?" I asked.

Scott paused. I could hear his breathing. "Meet me at the Marriott," he urged. His voice was weak.

I said, "I do not feel like going to the Marriott. We know Jaime is not there. Why? Can't you meet me at home?"

He insisted, "No, I need you to meet me at the Marriott."

I said, "Scott, if you know something, you need to tell me now!"

My friend paused and then began crying. "She's gone."

My world stood still. I was driving on the highway, and my wife, driving ahead of me, looked in her rearview mirror and could see I was getting emotional, so she called me. Before I could say anything, she said, "Who are you on the phone with?"

My voice was weak as I said, "Scott wants us to meet him at the Marriott."

"Why?" she pressed.

I explained that Scott had shared this was what law enforcement had requested. I did not want to tell her what I knew while she was driving on the highway. Jen didn't believe that I did not know something. She demanded that I inform her. I told her to pull over. On the side of the road, I had to tell my wife that our daughter had been killed.

Jaime became the first publicly identified victim.

It had been a few hours, and our friends were constantly calling. The news quickly ended up on Facebook. In twenty minutes, helicopters flew over my house and reporters began to call. Then they showed up at my door. Thank God I have police officer friends who provided security in front of my house for the next week to protect us from reporters. I ignored the media that whole week, but I've been very thankful for them since.

Scott knew from professional experience that the best way to make a death notification is face-to-face. That's why he'd tried to coordinate a spot where we could meet. But as soon as I heard his voice, I knew what he was trying to do.

Scott told his wife and daughter what had happened, attended a SWAT debriefing, and then came to our house, where his wife was waiting. My in-laws were there too. "You can't prepare for an incident like this," said Scott. "I became a part of the family."

When you experience the death of your child, the world stops. Everything you know and feel breaks into pieces. In the days following Jaime's murder, that's what I kept saying: "I feel broken." But I had a deep desire to know what had happened to my child. I am Jaime's dad. I will always be Jaime's dad. Though I couldn't function for myself, I had to do certain things for her, including listening to the description of her school being turned into a battlefield of terror and violence by one crazed coward with an AR-15 semiautomatic rifle. I had to hear how my daughter was hunted down and shot with one bullet in the side, severing her spinal cord.

Our lives were forever turned upside down by this six-minute murder spree of innocent teenagers and adults.

Almost immediately, we had to meet with law enforcement and make plans. Time stood still, yet at the same time, it marched forward with the reality that my wife and I needed to make funeral arrangements for Jaime. We needed security for our house and for the funeral, and Scott and other friends in law enforcement assisted with this. His family rode through the horror with us.

Amongst the many visitors in our house within twenty-four hours of this news were the girls that Jaime danced with; I call them her "dance sisters." Knowing that Jaime's favorite color was orange, they all came over wearing orange ribbons that night and went up to Jaime's room, where they posted photos. I did not realize it at the time, but for me, this was the beginning of our Orange Ribbons movement.

Later that night, around 9 p.m., Jen and I decided to kick everyone out of our house and go to the Marriott to be with the families waiting for news. Jesse came with us. It just felt like we needed to be with them, even though we knew about Jaime and they still had not been given confirmation of what had happened to their loved ones.

Details for me from that night are a blur. Apparently, I ran into Mayor Christine Hunschofsky, but the truth is that I do not remember doing so. We had just seen each other at a festive ribbon cutting a few days before. She recalls me saying that Jaime had been killed. She says even that night, she knew I was on a mission. She said I told her that I wanted to make sure this didn't happen to anyone again. I would do my part—somehow.

This chapter has been difficult to write, and, for the most part, it has been made up of my memories and point of view of the awful day. Jen had her own account of the day, which she wrote in an op-ed for *Newsweek* that ran on February 14, 2019, one year after the loss of our daughter.

One Year After the Day I Lost My Daughter to Gun Violence

By Jennifer Guttenberg

February 14. Valentine's Day. A day of love. Not in this town.

Exactly one year ago, Parkland, Florida, became another statistic. A former student came onto campus and killed seventeen students and injured seventeen others. One of the innocent victims was my fourteen-year-old daughter, Jaime Guttenberg.

That morning began like any other day: me repeatedly calling my two kids to get them out of bed, making their lunches, and rushing them out the door so they wouldn't be late. I kept their Valentine's Day cards and gifts for later that day so we could celebrate as a family. Out the door they went. They went to school. They went to learn. They went to be with their friends.

Only one of them came home.

I was working that day, as I often did. I am an occupational therapist and would travel from school to school and house to house, to help children who had special needs. I also ran an enrichment program in several preschools to help children with their fine motor skills and writing. This particular day, I had a class that I was teaching from 1:45 to 2:30. Little did I know that while I was teaching in a school just a minute up the road from my kids' high school, my daughter was being gunned down by a murderer. I was enjoying the three- and four-year-old children who were in my class that day. We laughed, we played, we learned, and we sang. I opened the door at 2:30 p.m., and the director of the preschool was standing in the doorway. I was startled as I didn't expect to see someone there. She quietly told me that they were in lockdown, and I followed her with the kids into another classroom. After dropping them off to a safe place, I proceeded

down the hall. A teacher was crying and scared;
she shrieked while asking me if I had a child at
MSD and told me there had been a shooting. I
was in disbelief. There have often been rumors
of threats to schools which turned out not to be
true. One by one, teachers became hysterical as
they received calls from their kids telling them
they heard gunshots and saw students who had
been shot. We attempted to turn on the TV, but it
wouldn't work.

My son called me. He was out of breath. He was
told to run as far away from the school as he could
go. He jumped a fence, scraping his leg, and ran.
As he was escaping, he also called my husband.
"Dad! Dad! There is a shooter at my school! And I
can't find Jaime!"

I then received another call from my son. He had
heard gunshots. He was running while calling
each of us every minute. Jaime wasn't answering
her phone. Nobody could reach her. I was in
lockdown at the preschool and couldn't get out.
Even if I tried to leave the roads were blocked off.
My husband got in the car and made his way to
the Walmart parking lot where he ended up…
along with the killer. They were all running away
from the school, *with the killer!* Nobody knew.
The police and the school thought he was still in
the building, but he was running right along with
the other students.

Once our son was home safely, my parents came to
be with him. We still needed to find Jaime. Social

media was blowing up with pictures of her, but people were quickly finding out that nobody had heard from her as they begged for any information on her whereabouts. There was a short period of time when someone said they had heard from Jaime, but it was a mistake. My relief once again turned into anguish.

Once I was allowed to leave the school, I jumped in my car, heart racing and head spinning, and made my way toward the hospital. My husband was heading there as well, while my son and parents headed to the hotel at which children who were safe were being dropped off to be reunited with their families. If Jaime was okay, they would be there for her. All I could think about was if she had been shot, I needed to be at the hospital with her immediately. I wasn't letting my baby girl lie by herself in a hospital with gunshot wounds.

We both arrived simultaneously and were escorted by the most caring and attentive hospital staff to a large room where we waited to hear our fate. We gave our daughter's name and showed them a picture of her. We had to do this several times with multiple people. They had some kids there who had not yet been identified. They gave us water and told us to drink as it's better to remain hydrated when you are hearing information that could be difficult. We waited and we waited. Seconds felt like minutes, minutes felt like hours. I was shaking. I felt sick.

Finally, someone came out and told us that Jaime wasn't there or at any of their other hospitals. It was also implied that there were still some kids unidentified at the school. My heart sank. Busload after busload of kids were dropped off at the meeting place, but still no Jaime. Friends were there waiting for her, but she hadn't come.

We each got back into our own cars, and at this point, I felt like I was hyperventilating. We had to get to the meeting place as fast as we could. My husband was calling every police officer he knew to see if anyone had seen her. My phone was ringing off the hook with friends wanting to know how they could help. There was so much traffic. We couldn't get there. My son and my parents couldn't get there either.

But it didn't matter. My husband spoke to a friend in law enforcement. He had seen her. She was gone.

My husband didn't want to tell me. He kept calling me and telling me to pull over and park so we could drive together. I just couldn't stop. I felt like I had to keep driving. My mind and body wouldn't let me stop. Finally, I could sense it in his voice. I begged him for the truth, and he told me.

We pulled over together. I got out of my car, screaming on the top of my lungs. I became hysterical and irrational. We had to tell our son and my parents. How could we? How would we? They were still trying to get to the meeting place, so we told them to come home, and we would meet them there. I drove home, blinded by my tears, barely able to breathe.

My husband and I arrived first. We waited in the driveway for them to pull up; when they did, I started screaming. It is still a blur, yet some parts are so clear. This was a nightmare from which we would never awaken. Within minutes, it seemed, the media found out and arrived at our home, looking for statements and answers. But they weren't getting any of that from us. Friends came to try to comfort us to no avail. We found out that all of the people who had not yet been reunited with their family members were awaiting knowledge of their fate at the hotel. We went there. We needed to hear the details of what had happened.

We arrived with our son and gave our information. The large banquet room, usually used to celebrate momentous occasions, was filled with terrified families and friends, desperately trying to find out if their loved ones were alive. We already knew. We also knew that nobody in that room was getting anything but bad news. You could just sense it. It was eerily quiet. There was food, water, and blankets provided by the Red Cross.

Nobody would talk to us. Nobody was willing to give us updates. It wasn't until around 1 a.m., 11 hours later, that the police and FBI came to tell us that they would be calling each family into a private room, one by one.

That was when the true nightmare began. The wails and screams were like no other. Fourteen students and three staff members were shot to death. How could this not be a dream?

But it was no dream. It has been one year since that day, a day that used to symbolize love, but turned out to be anything but. It hasn't gotten easier, it doesn't get better with time, and the pain never goes away. It will never be okay. It will never be fair. Seventeen wonderful, amazing people were taken that day. There were so many mistakes. I only wish I could turn back time. I wish my daughter had been sick that day as she had been the week before. I wish I could wake up from this nightmare. My family is forever broken. It will never be the same. This is how I feel one year later, so there is no need to ask.

We have a gun epidemic in this country and it must stop. It is a national emergency. If this can happen in a small, safe, upscale town like Parkland, it could happen anywhere.

Nobody should endure this kind of pain. Nobody should have to miss their child this much. I hope that every legislator reads this right after sending their kids to school. Or after sending them to the movies with their friends. Or even after dropping them off at a concert. *Then, maybe then, something will change.*

My wife is a very private person. Discussing any of this is very difficult for her. On the day that our daughter was shot, Jen was a helper to other kids who were in fear that they could be next.

While she does not talk about it, others have. Representative Jared Moskowitz made a very emotional speech on the floor of the Florida House on the day he was arguing on behalf of gun safety measures in Florida—legislation that was passed later that day. He talked about the reality that as Jaime was getting shot at her school, a fact that was not yet known to us, Jen was in a closet protecting and comforting Representative Moskowitz' son at the school where they were locked down.

Chapter 7

Unexpected Answers

The Parkland Vigil

Following a tragedy, you end up relying on others. Either people you know or new people you meet may become your helpers. Jen and I are so fortunate to have loving families and dedicated friends. With their help, we started to figure out what was next. Jen's parents live close by, and her brother and his family weren't far, either, and they came quickly. Jen's aunt and uncle and her cousins flew in from Texas. My siblings and their families flew to Florida the next day. My brother Ira flew in from North Carolina with his family, and Paul came from New York with his. My sister Abbie flew in from Cincinnati with her family and my parents. On the plane, my parents contemplated what had just happened to their fourteen-year-old granddaughter. They were supposed to be leaving soon for another cruise, and my spunky mother had been getting her nails done when she heard on the radio that there had been a shooting in Parkland.

My parents had just lost their son four months before. Imagine: In a period of just four months, my parents lost a son and a granddaughter. This is not the way life is supposed to work. Michael had been able to leave a legacy of many lasting achievements. He was fifty years old. Jaime was fourteen. She didn't have a chance to grow into the incredible person that everyone who knew her understood she was destined to become.

My two lifelong best friends came almost immediately. I grew up on Long Island with Jay Feinberg and Gary Ferber. I met Jay when we were in high school, while I've known Gary since we were toddlers; in fact, our mothers used to walk us together in our strollers. Jay came the day after Jaime's death and literally stood by my side, holding me together for days. Jay had been a cop in our community for twenty years and had also coached high school baseball for fifteen years. These ties to our community fueled his outrage over what had happened to Jaime and taken sixteen other innocent lives. I will always be grateful to him for getting me through the vigil, the funeral, and all the local media traffic.

On the flight to Florida, Abbie wrote a letter to "America" to express her rage. On her behalf, I can attest that she feels the emotions as strongly today as she did on that day.

She posted it on what had up to that point been her rarely used Facebook page, and it went viral before she even knew what "viral" meant. (Sadly, she now knows all about social media!)

Dear America,

We buried my brother, Dr. Michael Guttenberg, this past October. He was a 9/11 hero; sixteen years later he died of a 9/11 related cancer. Our country came together after the 9/11 terrorist attacks to overcome evil. We fought two wars, we subjected ourselves to onerous changes in air travel security, and we willingly gave up civil liberties to give ourselves the illusion of safety.

But we are not safe. This weekend we will bury my niece. Her name is Jaime Guttenberg, and she was the 14-year-old daughter of my brother Fred and sister-in-law Jen. She was Jesse's younger sister. Yesterday, she was murdered by a gun at her high school in Parkland, Florida.

Jaime was in the 9th grade. She was a pretty girl with the world's best smile, and her soul was sensitive and compassionate. She was intelligent and feisty, and she danced with beauty and grace. She always looked out for the underdog and the bullied, and she probably had been kind to the student who shot her. She planned to grow up and become a mom and a physical therapist.

Fred and Jen are the world's most loving and overprotective parents, but they could not protect Jaime from the sickness that has gripped our country. Unless we change, nobody can protect us. My friends and fellow citizens, your guns are not protecting you. Your guns are killing our kids.

Why is your hunting hobby more important than my niece's life? Don't you see that your "second amendment" rights have been twisted and distorted beyond any rational interpretation? Why should my niece have been sacrificed at the altar of your "freedoms?" Why don't you trust our police to protect us from crime? Don't you realize that mental illness has been and always will be a part of the human condition and that weapons of war should not be available to those among us who dream of mayhem and death? Don't you see the blood on all of our hands?

I don't care which shooter did this. If it had not been him, it would have been some other sad, sick, young man. I do care that he was able to legally purchase an assault weapon. I do care that the NRA and our so-called political leaders enabled him.

I don't care if the shooter spends the rest of his life in jail or gets the death penalty. That will not bring back Jaime, and it won't stop your kids from being the next victims of a "versatile, customizable"—and deadly—weapon of war. I do care that the NRA is dismantled. I do care whether our Congress and our President outlaw these technologically sophisticated tools of murder, just like every other civilized country on this planet. Failure to act will make our politicians complicit in Jaime's murder. I want them to face charges and I want them brought to justice.

My family does not want your thoughts and prayers. We want your action. Join us in fighting the NRA. Join us in deposing any politician who cares more about campaign contributions than for my beautiful Jaime. Join us in supporting leaders who will bravely fight for our children's lives.

Don't tell me not to politicize this. Jaime would want me to. This *is* political, and now, this is personal. If not now, when? If not us, who?

If we don't finally *act*, the sickness of gun violence will kill us all.

That Abbie's letter went viral so quickly became our first lesson in the power of social media. Understanding social media and its ability to reach an enormous audience far and wide would eventually become extremely important to my mission.

Amazingly, at this time, I was not even on Twitter. I didn't get an account until several weeks after the murder of my daughter.

For me, the moment that crystallized everything I do—the moment when I found my voice—wasn't the day my daughter was murdered—it was the next day, when I stood up at a vigil in Parkland.

I went to the vigil with Jesse, my sister, and family friends. Jen didn't go; she was in too much pain. I felt that I needed to be around people from the community. When I arrived to the sight of thousands of people from Parkland and other nearby communities, the mayor asked me if I wanted to speak. I was not prepared to make a speech, but I didn't hesitate for a second. I had a lot I needed to say. My speech went viral and was quickly felt around the country.

I did not go to this vigil prepared to speak, but when I went up to the podium and spoke, I was on fire. I talked about feeling broken. I cried out, telling the story of how I'd rushed my kids out the door the morning of the previous day as they were running late for school. I talked about how I could not remember if I had told Jaime "I love you" the last time I saw her. It was not supposed to be the last time. I was in a really raw emotional place. I also talked about the realization that my family and my community were victims of gun violence. That night became a defining night that set me on this path.

There's one way in and one way out of the park where the vigil was held. The scene was surreal. I had not expected to be asked to speak, nor for us to be showered with so much attention. We piled into Jay's truck, and he hopped curbs and worked with his friends in law enforcement to get us out of the park and home.

Like Abbie's letter, this speech, too, went viral. The next day I learned that Jaime's favorite actress, Zendaya, had shared it on social media, something Jaime would have been amazed to hear. I honestly cannot say if Jaime would have been more surprised by what I did in speaking out or by the fact that Zendaya was paying attention to her dad. My children know that I am always a fighter for them. I think Jaime would have been embarrassed by the attention. That said, I felt her with me that night, and with certainty I know she was standing on my shoulders and giving me the strength that I needed to stand up in front of that crowd. And she is giving me the strength that I need every day to go forward with being her voice and speaking out on her behalf.

***

We gradually discovered what happened in the last minutes of my daughter's life. She died in the hallway. The shooter worked his way up from the first floor. She was on the third floor. After shooting everyone he could inside, the shooter tried to blow out a window. Thank God it was hurricane-proof glass, so the bullets did not go through it. The shooter's intention was to shoot through the window at crowds of kids running for their lives. He had planned a Vegas-like mass murder spree involving killing many more people, but he failed at that.

The last picture that will ever be taken of my daughter was taken on the third floor of that school, with a black digital oval put over her body by law enforcement to hide her physical body.

We would soon learn that the Broward County Sheriff's Office, which had been in charge of the crime scene, had failed our families. There were communication issues. There were command and control issues. The school resource officer, a police officer with a gun, *hid*. The other officers who showed up knew what was happening in the school, yet they did not respond, allowing the shooter to continue with his deadly rampage without ever being confronted by law enforcement.

Over the course of the next few months, many groups and individuals would be identified as having failed to protect or respond, but the shooter is the only one who woke up that morning with the intention to kill. Unfortunately, we need to deal with the reality that human beings are capable of evil. We know this. That isn't new. But what I want to talk about is weapons. My daughter was killed while at school by a weapon of war by a teenage boy who was legally able to acquire that weapon.

My daughter's murder, together with the experience of giving a simple, unplanned speech the next day, changed my life. I hold guilt inside me over never having spoken up before after other shootings, after this happened to other people. If my voice is working now, maybe it could have worked then. Maybe if I had done something earlier, my daughter would be alive today. It's a guilt that I will live with for the rest of my life. The idea that I never fought like this when it was happening to other people's kids is something I will never get over. It is something that now moves me every second of every day: the need to fight for the safety of others. We *can* do more, and we *will* do more.

When I returned to the house from the vigil, I said to my wife and son, "I am going to break that fucking gun lobby."

I repeated this statement of my new mission throughout the week. My family is very politically engaged and extremely opinionated, so they all wanted to tell me how to do it. I am a pretty straight-down-the-line centrist. I call myself a pragmatist, but each family member wanted to share data, ideas, and *stuff*. I finally told everyone, "I don't want to know what anyone else does or try to turn myself into a policy wonk. I'm doing this my way." Truth is, I simply felt everyone involved in the issue up to that point had already failed, and I was not interested in legislators or legislation. I wanted to destroy the group that holds legislators and legislation hostage.

What my next steps would be and how I would move forward, I didn't yet know, but my friend Gary believed in me; he said, "Man, you'll figure it out! You said you needed a purpose after Michael died, now you have it." Gary knew me better than most, and he was right.

I did figure it out. I am Jaime's dad, and for me, the only thing that made sense was to do this as Jaime's dad. I am a father of two children, and what has carried me forward is the fact that I am reacting to what happened to one of my children. I don't claim to know more about the details of laws and their history than other people, but I am a dad who lost his daughter.

Nobody is trying to take guns away from lawful gun owners; however, we can do more to keep those who predictably will use guns for violence or to kill from having the access to do so. We will not stop all gun deaths, but we can significantly reduce the gun violence death rate. You're dealing with an industry that is kind of like tobacco. The tobacco industry managed to brilliantly control political decisions by throwing around loads of money so they could continue selling addictive, deadly products until, at last, they were forced to admit in a court of law that they knew the product was killing people and that it was addictive. We're at the start of the weakening and the downfall of the gun industry, but ultimately, it will require more successful elections, as well as lawsuits that will force the gun manufacturers into a court of law. Like the tobacco industry, they need to be made to admit what they knew when they made their decisions.

Chapter 8

Saying Goodbye

The last photo of Jaime

Two days after Jaime was killed, Jen and I went to the funeral home to plan our daughter's funeral. Jay, who did not leave my side, drove us, and Jen's parents also came with us. As we arrived to meet the rabbi and staff, Jay sat outside the room, giving us privacy, but staying close enough so that he could hear everything and ensure that I would not forget anything. Jen and I were clearly not in the place to concentrate.

The task of burying a loved one is grueling. When you are burying your child, the experience is simply indescribable. You never expect it, and you cannot plan for it in advance. Into this horrific mix came the funeral home staff, and their kindness was astonishing. They could not have been more accommodating

or compassionate—they were helpers in every sense. They did
not want us to worry about cost or any numbers and vowed
to take up the paperwork with the state. In the process of
talking to them and giving thought to how many people could
possibly be attending this funeral, given my daughter's place in
the community and the media coverage, we knew to expect an
enormous crowd.

While we were in that room going through details like what the
funeral would look like and who would give the eulogies, I kept
my phone on silent. Eventually, we took a break before choosing
a casket. I looked at my phone and saw a slew of text messages
and a voicemail from the FBI, all notifying me that they would
be holding a conference call with Parkland families who had lost
someone in the shooting. By the time I received these messages,
the time of the conference call had already passed, so I called
back. A woman informed me that since I had not been on the
group call, she could not disclose the news to me individually.
Well, needless to say, standing there in that somber funeral home
planning my daughter's funeral, I got angry.

"I demand whoever held that conference call get back to me to
tell me what I need to know." After a long pause, she agreed to
have someone return my call.

As we resumed picking out a casket, the FBI called back to tell
me "they had made a mistake." Approximately one month prior,
they had received information about the shooter to which they
should have responded, information that likely would have led
to the apprehension of the boy who went on to kill my daughter.
Unfortunately, the call center had not properly handled the
information, so there had been no follow-up action.

I was breathless. I finally gathered myself, stood up straight, and said, "Are you telling me that had the FBI done its job, my daughter would be alive today?"

He said, "I'm afraid so, sir."

The FBI had actionable intelligence before the shooting—they'd had the ability to have done something, and they failed. The failures of the FBI would soon become public in testimony from the FBI director as well as media coverage over the next few days. The FBI went public with their failure, but my recollection will always be this conversation, learning of the sobering reality that my daughter could have been saved, while looking at caskets for her final resting place.

After the funeral home, Jen and I went to the morgue to see our daughter. This was the first time that we could see her since she was murdered. I recall that she had a bruise on the side of her face from where she had fallen after being shot. It was covered with makeup, but I will never forget that bruise.

Jay brought us to the morgue and waited outside. I asked him if he wanted to say goodbye to Jaime. He said these were among the worst few moments of his life. This was coming from a man who had worked in general homicide and special victims units of law enforcement and had seen sick, injured, and deceased kids far too often. Jay always wanted to be in the special victims unit (SVU) because he figured that was the best way to protect kids. Seeing Jaime galvanized his efforts to protect my family and me.

One of the amazing things Jay did for us was he handled booking the venue for the funeral. We were concerned we needed a larger space than we'd first anticipated for all of the people we were expecting and told him so. "I'll handle it," he said, and he did. He went into the Coral Springs Marriott, and the Marriott offered their ballroom at no charge. "To this day," said Jay, "it still gets me emotional. I broke down when they offered a location, knowing how packed Jaime's service would be."

All I wanted Jay to do was shield Jen and Jesse. But he, like so many wonderful people, went above and beyond in the days, weeks, and months after our family was devastated by losing Jaime.

Before the mass shooting that killed my daughter, there had been the Columbine shooting. Sandy Hook. The Texas First Baptist Church massacre. The Las Vegas Strip. The San Francisco UPS shooting. Pulse Nightclub. The Aurora movie theater. Virginia Tech. The list of American cities and the number of bodies piled up is exhausting—and disgraceful, and sadly, continues to grow. Only three months after the Parkland shooting, the next mass school shooting happened in Santa Fe, Texas. We all remember the Pittsburgh Temple shooting in 2019, not to mention the weekend when two mass shootings happened, one in Texas and one in Ohio. There have been many others as well, furnishing further proof of how much at risk we still are. Each of these was also a reminder to me and my family of just how much we are now affected by *every* shooting. The weekend of the shootings in El Paso, Texas, and Dayton, Ohio, we were planning to go away for a few days on the weekend—the whole family. But because of the shootings, we just did not feel able to and postponed. A few days later, as we were traveling to go on vacation, I was on the phone for the entire drive with other people affected by gun violence, trying to discuss ways to do more and to do it faster. Sadly, at a national level, to this day, nothing has changed.

The conversation around how to keep America safe, or at least significantly safer, is too old and too long to cover in the pages of this book, but it is worth noting that *hundreds* of gun safety bills have been proposed since a gunman opened fire on Sandy Hook Elementary School in December of 2012, killing twenty children and six adults. Only a handful have actually become law. How can that be? We know all too well that with almost 400 million guns on the street now with more added every day, many of them are ending up in the hands of people who intend to kill.

Long before we met, Congressman Ted Deutch had been familiar with the kind of disturbing inertia that set in around the epidemic of gun violence in America. He has been a staunch advocate for common sense gun safety since 2010, the year he was elected to Congress, but he really stepped up after the events of February 14, 2018, in the 22nd District, which he represents.

Congressman Deutch was at a hearing in Washington when he received a text from one of his staffers. The staffer's daughter had texted her that there was a shooter at her school. The school was locked down, and she was hiding in a locker in the band room. Congressman Deutch left the hearing room immediately and called the sheriff, who was inside the school. The sheriff had already been inside and described it as "the worst thing that you could imagine." Congressman Deutch got a flight out late that night.

The next day, he attended the vigil. Then he attended as many funerals as he could in the coming days. He and his wife, Jill, came to our house during shiva, our weeklong period of honoring the five stages of mourning in Judaism. Their visit almost did not happen. I had made it clear to everyone that I did not want politicians coming to my home. Why? Because I felt that *all* politicians had failed on this issue, and the result was my daughter had been murdered. I was in a very emotional and angry place. My sister Abbie and Congressman Deutch's wife Jill have a mutual friend; My sister's friend reached out to Abbie to try to set up Congressman Deutch's visit. When Abbie told me about it, I said no. However, my sister, who was as always looking out for her brother, thought it would be a good idea and persisted. Eventually I agreed and said that they could come to my house, "for ten minutes."

When Congressman Deutch and his wife, Jill Deutch, arrived, Abbie and I met them at the driveway. As they politely expressed their sympathy, I launched into setting ground rules for their visit. While my memory is a blur, months later, Jill Deutch refreshed my recollection of what happened. While we can laugh about the memory now, I apparently put my finger right in Congressman Deutch's face, and the first thing I said was, "I am not interested in having politicians to my house this week. You have ten minutes." With my finger still pointing in his face, I went on to say, "This is my life mission now. My life mission is to haunt the halls of Congress and make sure that every single day, people are thinking about Jaime's name. You're either with me or I am going to be your worst enemy."

With total sincerity, Congressman Deutch replied, "Of course I am with you, as it's something that has always been important to me. I want to help you."

He reinforced that he would be there in this fight with his colleagues. With that, I shook his hand and invited them inside.

Jill reflects on that time as "one of the most painful nights of her life." "How do you comfort a grandparent, and a cousin, and a sibling, and a parent, for the tragedy of losing a fourteen-year-old child?" Though they were supposed to stay for only ten minutes, they stayed for hours and were the last to leave. My family and I fell in love with Congressman Deutch and Jill Deutch that night.

People often say politicians are the worst. This was my first experience with the opposite being true. Congressman Deutch stepped into my family's life because of Jaime's murder, but he has remained a part of our life in ways both public and private. He helped me to understand what this mission would look like and has provided me with any support needed as I went forward. For me, he is proof that people are inherently good, and he has been a true helper to me.

And so, my life now came to have many of these occasions in which grief by necessity had to merge with a goal. Feelings couldn't be fully processed without focus also being put on flashpoints of progress toward "destroying the fucking gun lobby." Death and loss had rapidly morphed into this mission. Grief is with me every single day, and my experience of grief is always the foundation of every day that I am on this mission.

On February 18, the day of Jaime's funeral, I woke up in a miserable place. Not surprising. I had written my eulogy the day before. My family and I were just trying to get through the hours before the funeral when someone alerted me to a tweet from the President about my daughter's murder:

Very sad that the FBI missed all of the many signals sent out by the Florida school shooter. This is not acceptable. They are spending too much time trying to prove Russian collusion with the Trump campaign—there is no collusion. Get back to the basics and make us all proud!

He politicized my daughter's murder. I would come to learn in the months following that by the time he put out this tweet, he had already met with the FBI about what had happened and knew the details of the FBI's failure. He knew it had nothing to do with Russia. He knew it had been a low-level call center failure, yet he chose to politicize my daughter's murder along with those of the other sixteen while we were still burying our loved ones.

Enraged, I started pacing the house while Jen urged me to calm down. We had to leave for the funeral in an hour. But I just couldn't ignore it. In that hour before leaving for the funeral, I sat down and rewrote the ending of my eulogy with a direct response to the President's tweet, along with a request. The only thing this man should have been doing then was reaching out to determine what he could do to prevent this kind of violence from happening again.

An estimated 2,000 people attended Jaime's funeral, with at least a thousand inside the Marriott and many more outside. I remember driving up to the Marriott and seeing a lot of fire trucks and firefighters in full dress uniform. My son was (and still is) a member of the Broward Sheriff Fire Cadets. Emergency service vehicles came from all over to let Jesse and our family know that they were there for us, for anything we would need. The thing about helpers is that they can show up unexpectedly. For my son, this act of kindness and love from the first responder community was something that helped him get through the hardest day of his life. My gratitude to these amazing men and women will go on forever.

Once inside, we were escorted to a private room; then a few minutes later, prior to the funeral, we were escorted to the casket to spend our final moments with Jaime. After some time with her, we were told it was time to start the funeral and the casket was closed. That was the last time I ever saw my fourteen-year-old daughter's body—the last time I ever glimpsed her face.

My eulogy was mostly about Jaime, but was also an appeal to everyone listening to do more.

> "I was never a voice in the gun violence debate before, but I will be now. Let me be clear, I have been triggered. With you by my side, I will fight. For those of you who do not know me and what I can be like when I take on a cause, I will be relentless. This will be my life's cause going forward. The Orange Ribbon Movement started by Jaime's beautiful dance sisters in Parkland, Florida, will become the rallying cry for the fight against gun violence. We will win, and we will be able to safely send our kids to school.

> If you do not agree with me, I simply ask that you stand with me in a move for improved public safety and an understanding that my daughter was killed by a gun. This could have been your kid. This cannot continue. Nobody can tell me that gun violence does not exist and that we do not have a public safety issue. My family is broken because of it. Thank you all for your love and outpouring of support. In spite of this tragedy, it reaffirms my faith in humanity. We love you all."

Following this, I went on to deliver the newly written ending to my eulogy, in reply to the President's tweet, ending with a request.

> "I need to say one more thing. I heard about presidential tweets this morning linking my baby's death to the Russia probe. The FBI made a

tragic mistake, it needs to be dealt with. But [Mr.
President,] I have not even heard from you. You
are not going through what my wife and I are going
through, and you do not have my permission to pull
my daughter's death into the Russia probe. What
happened here in Parkland has nothing to do with
it, and it needs to be dealt with in a non-political
way, one that accurately deals with the issue of gun
violence so that we can safely send our children to
school. You do have my permission, if you would
like, to join me in this fight for public safety and
all that it includes, such as mental health, which we
agree on, and the weapon of choice, which happens
to be guns."

In closing, I turned around and hugged the rabbi as my tears
started to fall. When I turned back around, everyone was on their
feet. I hit my heart with my fist to acknowledge the support and
then turned around again, holding the rabbi and my wife, all of
us sobbing.

The President's insensitive and widely broadcast message outraged
a great many people, as was widely reported. For me, it reinforced
that this President would be a non-factor in any alliance in my
path going forward. I came to the realization that he was certainly
going to be an obstacle when he refused to say the word "guns"
while talking about a mass shooting. If you talked about the
Parkland massacre and school security but didn't say the word
"guns," you were making yourself irrelevant to me. He refused to
say the word all week.

Jen gave a eulogy. She generally does not speak in front of crowds,
but anyone who knows my wife knows that when she speaks, you
need to stop and listen. Her eulogy was emotional from start to

finish, and I think it left the entire crowd of 2000 sobbing. How could it not? Jaime's best friend and cousin also spoke, as did one of Jaime's teachers. The rabbi could not get through the words he had written without his voice cracking. In that moment, his message to everyone in that room was not a religious message, it was deeply personal, and one that has continued to resonate with me every minute of every day since. "We don't move on," he said. "We move *forward*."

There isn't a second that I'm moving on without my kid, but I am moving forward with her on one shoulder and my brother on the other.

Chapter 9

Gathering Ammunition

At the CNN Town Hall

After focusing on my child's burial and spending the week in my house grieving, I attended the infamous CNN Town Hall on gun violence in America. A few friends and some family, including my son Jesse, joined me. Jen stayed back at the house with other friends and family, as they were not yet up to going out. For those who stayed back home to watch it, they were witnesses to a very unusual and surreal moment, one which for us was our first sign from Jaime.

Our puppy, only a few months old, was sitting on the couch with everyone who stayed home to watch the Town Hall. When CNN flashed a picture of Jaime on the screen, the puppy howled so long and in such a visceral way that Jen and everyone else in the house freaked out. The sound of that shrieking cry at the sight of her picture is something that they will never forget. He never made that sound ever again.

Senator Rubio refused to say the word "guns" for the entire week leading up to the Town Hall with Jake Tapper. Senator Rubio expressed that he was coming to face this crowd with the knowledge that it was hostile; he wanted to lay out his positions in the hope that people would end up liking him.

I started my questions to him by acknowledging his desire to be liked. I told him that I wanted to like him. I also told him that his inability to say the word "guns" made him sound pathetically weak and made it hard for me to like him.

I went on to ask him, "You have not said 'guns' all week. Will you stand here and say tonight that guns were the reason that this happened?"

He did not. It was becoming clear that during this battle, there would be times when I would need to conserve some of my energy, as it was becoming clear to me just how entrenched some of these people were. If Senator Rubio wanted to kowtow to the NRA on prime-time TV, and by so doing, make himself look completely out of touch with what had just happened to constituents in the state he represents—in fact, literally in his backyard, since we live only about thirty miles from his home—he would have to pay in lost voter support at election time.

The CNN Town Hall kicked off the nonstop part of what I do.

The following morning, I appeared on "Morning Joe" with Joe Scarborough and Mika Brzezinski for over twenty agonizing minutes. I believe we had only been scheduled for about five minutes. Mika and Joe were sincerely interested in what had happened to Jaime, and they gave me the opportunity to share my story in a very personal way. As I was practically in tears for the whole segment, they shared my agony. Over the course of the following months' appearances on both MSNBC and CNN, my respect for the media grew. The journalists I met were fair and wanted me to be able to share my story, and I am thankful for their consideration in providing me, as well as others, a platform to talk about this issue.

Unfortunately, I have never appeared on Fox News. They haven't invited me. I tried, though, because I think that audience should hear both sides of this issue. In fact, in 2018 at Politicon, I gave my card to Tucker Carlson, explaining that I had not received an invitation to appear on Fox. I told him that I would like to speak with their audience as well and would be happy to go on his show. He said he would schedule something. I never heard back.

When I started doing this work and giving interviews, as well as going to meet with legislators in Washington, DC, I would refuse to sit down. When I considered the other instances of gun violence before Parkland, the reaction to each of those events was way too comfortable, way too polite, and way too temporary. I had no need or desire to make people feel comfortable.

Often, I'd visit senators and congressmen in their offices, and they would tell me to have a seat.

I would say, "No. I don't need to be comfortable when I talk about my daughter. You can sit, or you can stand with me." Standing became symbolic for standing up for Jaime. I learned that to be effective in your speech, no matter the audience, stand when everyone is sitting. It leaves an impact.

A couple of them chose to sit down. One of the congressmen, rather than sitting behind his desk, sat *on* his desk. But as I was telling him the story of how Jaime died, I didn't feel I was making a connection with him; I just did not feel he was truly engaged. At the moment that I described her being hit by a bullet, I ended up slamming my hand on the desk to mimic the sound of a bullet. He jumped. That moment changed how I talk about Jaime being murdered, and it is now always part of how I talk about what happened. It scares the daylights out of people, but they better understand the suddenness, the brutality of it.

I testified before a Senate subcommittee about what happened, standing the whole time and happy to explain why when they asked. I also referred to the NRA's behavior as "terror-like;" this became a news story that day. The NRA had just put out a video with the title, "Times Up" that talked about putting targets on the backs of political leaders and entertainers who disagreed with them. That night, I did a town hall with Congressman Deutch and Congressman Don Beyer from Virginia. I stood through all of that Town Hall as well. By the end of the day, I had stood for about fifteen hours straight. Upon returning to my hotel, I thought my legs were going to fall off. Even while I was exhausted, I stood up for Jaime and have not stopped standing for her since.

Jaime used to always mess with my phone, and one thing she did was place entries on random dates throughout my calendar that said, "Love Jaime Day." It was like Valentine's Day on steroids when one of those days would come up. I never looked at when one was going to happen; it would just surprise me with a calendar reminder on my phone. Usually, she would be in school when I got this reminder, then I would text her, and that would be the start of Love Jaime Day.

On March 6, while I was on my very first visit to DC following Jaime's murder, I was walking into the Rayburn congressional office building when a calendar reminder showed up: It was Love Jaime Day. I simply fell apart and sat outside crying. My day almost ended before it could even start.

After crying for some time, I pulled myself together because I knew I had work to do. I realized that this was a sign from Jaime: She was with me as I was about to begin fighting for her.

Later that morning, I visited with Senator Rubio. We picked up where we had left off at the CNN Town Hall, talking about the need to do more for gun safety and the money that he receives from the NRA. I wish I could tell you that this visit changed something between us. It did not. In fact, this was the day that the Florida House was debating and ended up passing the gun safety measure approved by the Florida Senate on the previous day. We already knew the Republican governor would sign it. I tried to get Senator Rubio to publicly support this gun safety bill. I even suggested that we do a press conference suggesting he could get behind this. But he refused, and that was the end of our conversation. I took it as a blatant example of how NRA money works to cause legislators like him to fail at doing their job. We have since spoken several additional times; however, I do not expect him to change or to be someone I can count on for support for public safety.

Chapter 10

Orange Ribbons for Jaime

Me being greeted by Joe Biden at the presidential debate in Miami

At only fourteen years of age, my daughter stood up for other people who couldn't stand up for themself. That is how she lived her life. When I feel like I am being pushed to the limit, I think of her.

Jaime was born with the tough gene. She did not put up with normal kid nonsense. She didn't put up with others being treated poorly. She died running for her life and made it to within one second of safety as she was turning toward the shelter of a stairwell when a bullet hit her. The idea that she was fighting for her life until her final second does not surprise me. I have Jaime and Michael, the two toughest people in my life, standing on my shoulders and pushing me forward, so I can do what I have to do now. That they both would never hesitate to put the safety of others above their own is now how I will go forward living my life.

Jaime dreamed of working as a pediatric physical therapist and regularly volunteered her time to work with kids with special needs. She truly had a special touch and a caring approach with these kids. One, a former neighbor, is on the autism spectrum. Jaime was one of the few people besides his parents, who could connect with him. She would babysit him so that his parents could take a night off. He was very affected by Jaime's murder. He doesn't show a lot of emotion, but he clearly articulated his sadness.

Because of my wife's work as a pediatric occupational therapist and Jaime's unfulfilled plan to follow in her footsteps as a pediatric physical therapist working with special needs children, we dedicated a dance room at a community center to kids of all abilities. It's now being used to hold dance classes in Jaime's name. At the opening dedication ceremony, several of us spoke. The boy Jaime used to babysit attended with his parents; he surprised everyone as he stepped up and announced he wanted to say something. He gave this unbelievably heartwarming speech about what Jaime had meant to him. It was the most emotional he had ever been, and his parents were crying as well. I felt that Jaime was talking through him.

My memories of Jaime's toughness are plentiful. Even in such a short life, what she did affected so many people. When she saw bullying happening at school, she had a big problem with it and would insert herself directly into the middle to make it stop. Sometime after Jaime's death, a teenager approached my wife and me and explained that though she had been bullied in years past,

Jaime would not allow anyone to harass her when they attended the same school.

At the age of twelve, Jaime came home from middle school one day and described how she had stood up to a big bully that was bullying another person, complete with details of the bully's large size. Afraid that my daughter would come home with a black eye, I tried to discourage her from getting into the middle of physical altercations. I told her it would be better if she got the adults at the school to handle it.

Jaime smirked and responded, "Dad, don't underestimate me because of my size!" Jaime truly believed she was the toughest person in the room.

Jokingly, in that moment, I put my hand out towards her shoulder and pushed her. She pushed me back. I pushed her again, and then I got what became known as the "kangaroo kick" in my house because she had these fast, strong dancer's legs, and she was going to end it right there. When I got my bearings again, I simply put my hand on her shoulder and told her, "I should be really upset with you, but if someone ever tries to hurt you, do what you just did to me!"

I wear an orange ribbon each day in honor of Jaime. Several weeks after Jaime's murder, a stranger walked up to me and asked me about it. After I told him why I was wearing it, he explained to me that it was also the color of the gun safety movement. I had not known this until that moment. The connection between Jaime's favorite color and the gun safety movement inspired me to start the organization, Orange Ribbons For Jaime, to honor our daughter by supporting programs that were important to Jaime in life, as well as to take action to deal with the underlying cause of why her life was cut short. I now spend time traveling the country educating people on common sense gun safety. I am truly touched as I see the Orange Ribbons For Jaime pins being worn across the country. The actor Bradley Whitford bought his over a year ago and wears it every day since to honor Jaime and the victims of gun violence. He is another unexpected helper.

I met him in person in 2018 at Politicon in California. He was on a *West Wing* reunion panel with the cast, and political commentator Lawrence O'Donnell was moderating. While I stood at the right side of the room, to my surprise, O'Donnell mentioned me in an answer to a question. Bradley Whitford jumped out of his chair and started tugging on his shirt to show me he was wearing his Orange Ribbons For Jaime pin.

We spoke afterwards, and he went on to tell me that he thinks of Jaime all of the time and that he would do anything he can to support the fight for gun safety. He did not know it at the time, but I'd been feeling discouraged. I had good days, and then I had terrible days. Seeing him wearing this pin inspired me greatly, as it let me know that people across the country were paying attention and were supportive of what I was trying to do. Unexpectedly encountering him like this gave me the energy to keep going.

My family has been part of two distinctly American tragedies. Following 9/11, this country made changes to ensure a tragedy like that would never happen again. We changed the way we fly, and we added a Department of Homeland Security. With gun violence so common in the US, it is a national terror. I intend to play a part in ensuring this country does something about it. As such, working to eliminate gun violence is my life mission, and one that truly dominates every encounter since then.

I grew up in a house where the news was on…*all* the time. We all read the newspaper and knew what was going on. I imagine my daughter would have followed in the same vein. My mother had gotten involved with Moms Demand Action for Gun Sense in America after Sandy Hook, as she couldn't believe there was no real legislation addressing what had happened. In one sense, Abbie writing her "Dear America" letter didn't surprise me, but in another it did: Before posting her letter, Abbie was a very private person. She had signed up for Twitter at the insistence of her kids but rarely went online. Once her open letter was made public, she received messages from places as far away as Australia, New Zealand, and everywhere around the world, sending her their support. Abbie had quickly learned what "going viral" meant.

The first day I joined Twitter changed everything for me. The problem I had with writing tweets was that with their 140-character limit per tweet, you have to write things so concisely! But I started tweeting and quickly figured out how to write shorter and more impactful messages. People across the country in media, politics, and entertainment were paying attention, and they started to follow me. Twitter became my voice. Being an influencer brought me a ton of followers who were working toward the same cause, but naturally, it also drew a level of negativity that I had not previously experienced.

I always used to tell my kids, "You have to accept people for who they are. You cannot worry much about what others say or do. You can only worry about your own choices and decisions." In that spirit, I resolved that I would simply not worry myself over the negativity. I chose to only worry about my own statements. While this was always a philosophy I believed in, that doesn't mean it was easy to live by. Honestly, the day that Jaime died, my ability to be worried about or impacted by negativity and fear died with her. And what was hard—dealing with not being liked—became easy.

My fight for gun safety has defined my life since February 14, 2018, but this life is not for everyone. My wife does not want this kind of life for herself, but she understands why I do it. She is a very private person who is angry that our lives together have changed so drastically, that our lives no longer involve dance competitions and the silly laughter that was our normal everyday experience with Jaime. Instead, our life now involves this mission of doing something about what happened to our daughter. She is upset that we need to do this, and she is angry that the failures that created this could have and should have been addressed long ago. She is upset that we now talk about our daughter in the past tense.

Being in the public eye is not something in which Jen has any interest, so for the most part, she does not get involved in public advocacy. But when she does write or speak, pay attention! It is always powerful and emotional.

When I think about how Jen and I have been grieving in sometimes different ways, I always think about what Vice President Biden said to me during our first conversation. "Everybody goes through grief differently," he told me.

He first called me just ten days after Jaime died. I don't know how he knew how to reach me, but I was moved. We talked for almost an hour; mostly, he asked questions. He wanted to know more about Jaime, Jen, and Jesse, and more about me. He asked what kind of interests the kids had and what kind of work my wife and I do. At one point, I said to him "I want to break that fucking gun lobby," and what followed between us included some colorful language. It felt like a call with an old friend who cared and was following up. It was so comfortable and comforting. As most everyone knows, this is a man who has experienced great tragedy in his life. He spoke to me with so much empathy and understanding, I felt like I'd known him forever.

A few weeks later, a Parkland resident I had gotten to know following Jaime's murder who also had a connection to Vice President Biden called to tell me the Vice President would be in West Palm Beach holding a fundraiser for the Beau Biden Foundation. My friend invited another Parkland dad and me to the fundraiser at the request of Vice President Biden. When the day of the fundraiser arrived, the other dad and I were only expecting a five-minute meeting as the Vice President had a few hundred people waiting to see him. But when he was done shaking hands with the attendees, he called us into a private room where he spent about forty-five minutes with us. About twenty minutes into the meeting, I reminded him that he had a room full of people waiting to hear from him. He said, "Don't worry, this is more important," and went on to comfort us. He talked to us about mission and purpose and how that had helped him to get through his own grief. This discussion has played a big role in forming my path forward.

He also told me that the time will come, both for my wife and me and for Jesse, when the memories of Jaime will bring a smile to our faces and maybe even laughter instead of tears. He told me to give it time, that we would all get there. He was right.

I remember him again talking about grief and how we all grieve differently, telling us, "You can't try to force someone to go through it the way you are going through it. You have to find ways to grieve in your own unique way, while at the same time continuing to be supportive of one another." He wanted us to know that *now* so we would be prepared, so that we could create a plan to make sure the relationships with those we love the most would survive. He was the first person to bring this up with me.

He wanted me to understand the challenges of grieving and how being prepared would help our families to get through the days and months ahead. He gave me the advice that I needed, and it has made an enormous difference.

I won't forget the sincerity in his voice. I won't forget that moment of solidarity. He is a man who understands loss and grief, and his words will resonate with me forever. For those who stay on the quieter side and need their privacy, I get that. For those like me, and like some of the other parents and kids who have fought, I get that, too. Something else I always told my kids was, "You do what you think is right. Don't question it too much. Don't be influenced by others who may try to convince you of the opposite. If you do what you believe is right, you'll always be okay. You will always be able to look back and know that you did the right thing, something that you believed in." That's what I'm doing now. On social media, I get beat over the head every day, but I believe that what I am doing is right, and no one will change my mind on this.

Those who believe they need to be quieter, that it will be more beneficial for them and those they love in the long term, are doing what is right for them. For me, what feels natural and right is to continue being Jaime's dad in this way. As parents, we always react to what happens to our children. This mission is how I will continue being a father to both my children, to both Jesse and Jaime.

In the weeks following Jaime's murder, I began to become familiar with large advocacy groups like The Brady Campaign, Giffords Courage, and Everytown for Gun Safety. I also got to know some smaller groups to which I felt a deep connection. I became closely connected with the work being done by the Newtown Action Alliance, Guns Down America, CeaseFirePA,

Change The Ref, and others. I chose not to align with any single group but to work with all of them. I chose to go forward as Jaime's dad and to bring my emotion with me every single day. I wanted to remind everyone what it means to be a victim of gun violence, to be the father of a daughter who was murdered by an AR-15 while she was at school. My mission was not about becoming a policy expert. I wanted to figure out how to build alliances with these groups, as well as groups on the other side of the issue, with the hope of creating the conversations needed to lower the gun violence death rate.

The dad in me wants to appeal to both sides. Guns don't discriminate; bullets don't discriminate. When they hit you, they do not know if you are a Republican or Democrat. They do not know if you are for or against gun safety. They don't know if you are black or white. When they hit you, all that you know is that they are likely to kill you.

My family became more deeply involved in my mission. Even my brother Paul, not usually one to engage in public speaking, gave speeches at numerous rallies and events. Like me, he's met some amazing people, though unfortunately all for the wrong reasons— because they're victims of gun violence or had loved ones killed in the Parkland mass shooting, like the Beigel family. Scott Beigel was a teacher at Parkland, and his parents live in New York near where Paul lives. They've spoken at the same events in an effort to bring positive change, and Paul has become passionate about doing so, even though like all of us, he gets frustrated.

"I never knew what a lockdown drill was," he told me when he was particularly agitated one day. "When I went to school, we had fire drills. Today, these kids live in a different world. They're living in a different reality, and adults who care about kids need to realize that these kids are growing up to be trained to jump under a desk or into a closet. Schools are being turned into prisons."

I often wonder if we think enough about the mental aftermath of these violent, life-altering events. Do we reflect upon how young people go on with images of terror and death forever imprinted in their psyches? Or how families try to go on in the same home that was once filled with the youth and vibrancy of their loved one? In my case, Jaime was the energy in our home. We were always laughing or yelling because of her, always responding to her. My home is a much quieter place since Jaime's voice was silenced.

We will never stop every shooting, but we can stop many of them and we can do something about the amount of bullets or the type of weapons somebody can buy, and we can work to transform the environments that produce killers. That nineteen-year-old should not have had access to an AR-15. If we can save one life in a bad situation, that one life could be a family member of yours, and wouldn't that be an amazing thing?

"I will never sleep comfortably again knowing what happened and where this country is," Paul said. "I've always been a very political person, but I am a one-issue person now. We need to correct this. That their guns are more important than 40,000 lives lost per year to gun violence makes no sense to me."

I never imagined that my entrepreneurial background would make me well suited to activism or to building our foundation, Orange Ribbons for Jaime, but here we are.

While other kids were leaving college and looking for jobs, I had already developed entrepreneurial interests. Even before I turned ten, I used to go around the neighborhood and take people's junk like bicycles and lawnmowers that they didn't want. Then I'd fix and resell them. My dad bought me a junk car when I was fourteen, and I learned how to work on it. Then I started buying and selling cars.

In high school and college, I used to take people to buy cars because no one knew how to engage with a dealership. I had already figured out how to negotiate. In college, I wrote a business plan to take automotive retailing out of the dealership. This was in the mid to late eighties. My plan even included using this new thing, "the Internet," for buying and selling. I believed so strongly in my plan that I wanted to drop out of college.

My dad said no chance.

I kept being a pain in the ass about it, so he took me to see a customer of his who owned auto dealerships. "If Arnold thinks there is any merit in this, I'll let you sit out a semester." Upon hearing my idea, Arnold put his hand on my shoulder and said, "Son, no one will ever buy a car without sitting in the seat and kicking the tires."

My dad said, "Exactly! Go back to school." As we all know now, he was wrong, and automotive retailing outside of the dealership has become a huge business. I just needed a phone and a computer. I regretted not pursuing this dream, which was part of why I raised my kids to always follow their passions and interests.

I graduated from Skidmore College in 1988. After college, rather than finding a normal job, I bought an automotive detailing business. A year in, I realized I'd made a mistake. It was a mostly cash business. I was young and didn't have a moment to myself—I was just working nonstop, and I didn't spend any time with friends. My brother Michael's college graduation was coming up, and I almost couldn't go because of the business. That near-conflict prompted me to sell the business and move to Florida.

I'd first visited Florida with Jay when I was a junior in high school; we stayed at his grandmother's. As we landed, I was struck by the greenery and sunshine. I'd wanted to live there ever since. When I sold the business, the decision to move to Florida was an easy one. As I was moving there without a job, Michael took over the purchase of my brand-new car so that I would not have that expense. A friend's parents owned a house in Palm Beach, and they needed to have a car driven there. I drove down in that car and used it until I bought a used car for myself. I arrived in Florida in September of 1989 with everything I could fit in that car. I settled in the city of Plantation because the apartment complex boasted a free washer and dryer. I filled the place with used furniture and never looked back.

Two years later, while running up credit card debt as I was not making enough money, I called my dad and informed him that I'd made a decision to return to New York.

"Why?" he asked. "You're happy there."

This was true, but I explained I could no longer afford my lifestyle.

Then he asked, "Where are you going to live?"

I said, "I'm moving back in with you and Mom."

"No, you are not," he said. "If you need money, ask for that, but you need to stay where you're happy."

It was a great parenting moment. He would not let me quit living in Florida if I was happy. I listened to him. Less than two weeks later, I was hired by Johnson & Johnson and worked there for fourteen years, climbing higher and higher up the ranks until I left in 2004 to start my own Dunkin' Donuts business.

Being a sales professional and then owning a franchise is not necessarily what usually leads to the making of an activist. But the skills I developed over my years of work have certainly been useful in my current mission. My ability to communicate and organize myself has been invaluable. As an entrepreneur, I certainly learned how to do a lot with limited resources, which also has been invaluable in this mission.

Intense tragedy and loss change your framework for how you live your life. I know that life is fragile and can end at any moment. Because of what happened, I live every day now with the understanding that there may not be a tomorrow. I also know that I could become the next victim of gun violence before the end of the day. I used to dream of and plan for the future. I don't anymore. I know all too well that in a split second, everything can end. My vision is day to day. Strangely, having a day-to-day vision has made me nimble, able to react to moments as they happen and plan accordingly.

Chapter 11

Uncommon Alliances

The Kavanaugh handshake

Around 2:15 in the morning the night after Jaime was killed, my son came down the stairs hysterical. What had triggered it was something quite simple. Jesse and Jaime shared a bathroom. Every night, there would be an argument over that bathroom; it was normal sibling stuff and no big deal.

However, when he came downstairs to us that night, Jesse said, "She didn't fight back."

The reality of losing his sister finally hit Jesse in that moment—the reality that he was now an only child and would never be an uncle was overwhelming for him.

In the six or so weeks that followed, his hockey teammates and friends did not let him go. Outside of Jen and me, they were his support system. Every chance he could, he went out with them. They lifted him up at the time in his young life when he needed them most. For Jesse, his friends and his hockey team became his team of helpers in the most amazing and needed ways.

While my roles as husband to Jen and father to Jesse were needed in my home more than ever, my travel and activities ramped up because of what happened to Jaime. I was traveling all over. Never before had there been such a surge in support of legislation to prevent gun violence in the United States.

We all watched as the courageous kids from Parkland ignited a flame and started the March for Our Lives. I knew many of these kids before the shooting, and I was truly stunned to see how it changed them. I have been vocal about how I did not see this teenage leadership coming—I used to think they were all so focused on their phones and social media, but I did not realize just how well they could communicate. Thankfully, I was wrong; the phone became their weapon. They are phenomenal communicators, fierce in demanding what they want, and they use that phone to organize and to galvanize support for their aims. The March they led is one for the history books. Hundreds of thousands of people gathered in Washington to call for tighter gun laws following the massacre. These young activists from Parkland and across the country led the rally in an array of powerful and composed speeches. Children, students, and parents walked out of hundreds of schools across the country at the same time.

When we were led in six minutes and twenty seconds of silence by Emma Gonzales to symbolize the amount of time the shooter had taken to kill seventeen people, my whole body was filled with an odd mix of sadness and rage—such a tiny slice of time, yet such destruction. When I learned that President Trump had spent the day of the March at his golf club in Florida, I was just livid.

From the moment that I started on my mission, I never felt alone. I was astounded by how many people cared so much about the issue of gun violence. Alyssa Milano and Ben Jackson started a group called NoRA and invited me to join them at a protest they were organizing outside of the National Rifle Association (NRA) convention in Dallas, only a few weeks after the march on Pennsylvania Avenue. I am proud to call Alyssa and Ben my friends, friends who have never wavered in either their public or private support of my family and me.

Alyssa was a fifteen-year-old idol starring on the show *Who's the Boss?* when she got her first taste of the power of activism. Elton John called to introduce her to Ryan White, also a teenager, who had contracted HIV through a blood transfusion. "There was a lot of stigma surrounding HIV," Alyssa remembered. "He was HIV positive at a time that HIV [was thought to have] a very distinct look that he did not resemble. He was kicked out of school." Alyssa was in awe of him. "He invited me to go on *The Phil Donahue Show* and allow him to kiss me so we could make people aware that you could not contract HIV through casual contact. I said yes. I went on the show. He kissed me. Together, we changed the narrative. From that moment on, I realized what having a platform meant and what a responsibility it was. It gave me a direction I don't know I would have necessarily had, though I was politically and socially aware. I realized what I was capable of. It gave me more motivation to continue acting, even.... When we talk about how one person can make a difference and humanize the issue, that is exactly what Ryan White did. I'm an actress. I'm a storyteller. Results come from humanizing the issue."

What Alyssa did was fearless. For me, fear died on the day my
daughter died. I knew that in order to carry out my mission,
I needed to be fearless. Perhaps that is why we connected
so quickly.

Activism takes storytelling, but I've learned that it also takes guts.
You have to be fearless, because you're going to create division
and piss people off. When NRA members and supporters showed
up and surrounded the park in Dallas with their guns and
megaphones, I admit to feeling both angry about the weapons
and amused by the megaphones. When they surrounded the park
and tried to talk over us, I acknowledged them and continued
with my speech. I jokingly told the protesters that when red flag
laws come to Texas, I predicted that they would all lose their
weapons. When they realized that they could not stop me from
speaking, they left. ("Red flag" laws, or Extreme Risk Protection
Orders (ERPOs), allow family members, police, or other third
parties to ask the court to temporarily remove a person's guns if
it is believed there is a high degree of risk of that person being
violent. If the court judges that person is dangerous to himself
or others, then he must surrender all firearms to the police for a
specific period of time. During that period, the person is also not
allowed to buy or sell guns.)

I shared photos of Jaime at the event. I wanted people to react, to
be emotional; I wanted people to feel my pain, and to think about
it like moms and dads. Alyssa was approached by this group of
guys with guns who were harassing her and giving her a hard time
for being an activist with armed security. Alyssa conducted herself
with integrity, honesty, and decency in response, and answered
everything they said by engaging in civil discussion. Within hours
that day, the NRA had posted a video trying to make it look like
Alyssa and her security were harassing them. I had been part of
that story, so I knew the truth. Immediately, I started going after

every single thing they were saying. Using social media, we were able to make sure we put out the truth.

The NRA Convention proved to be more than a group of guys with guns harassing us and screaming in our faces. It actually inspired me to be more aware and better prepared. The whole disgusting scene made me more determined to be my daughter's voice, a voice of good and humanity. There were scary moments in that dangerous setting. Just thinking of all that ammunition and firepower out in the open, I cringe.

Ben shares what he learned that day, which is like a rare glimpse into the belly of the beast: "I saw a lot of people there who had lost somebody, and I saw a lot of personal, righteous anger. As far as many NRA members, once you get past the initial resistance and you can talk about the things you believe, there is a surprising amount of common ground. The NRA membership is different from the NRA leadership. Even though you don't agree on everything, there is room for middle ground. That's important to find out because it changes whom your messaging is targeted to. You can talk to members about the leadership and make a distinction between the two."

But to be clear, we also saw a bunch of idiots.

As Ben put it, "People think that it's really okay to walk the street with assault weapons out and displayed, wearing paramilitary uniforms and camouflage, because they can—and they want to intimidate people. We saw a demonstration of a lot of very armed people who were precisely the people that shouldn't be armed or using guns as props to scare people. It defined for us how entrenched some of this opposition is going to be. It was a little scary! …There was a young woman who had been a Parkland student and was handing out literature. The way these guys spoke to her was hateful, sexual, and demeaning. A crowd of heavily armed guys got in our faces. There were a lot of guns and a lot of tempers. If these people had been alone and unarmed, they never would have behaved like this. It was eye-opening as to what this convention and these guns bring out in the people likely to behave like this. That has a lot of potential for things to go wrong. The police had to come in and haul out this crowd. I'm a Navy veteran and have fired every weapon you can fire. I do know what these guns do. I don't spook easily, but when you have this type of person with a gun bearing down on you and screaming, it's a lot to face."

Most people agree that every person who obtains a gun should go through a background check and shouldn't have a gun in their hands until that check is complete. And in Dallas, people told us they'd be willing to do that and also said the armed groups roaming around were hurting their cause and not helping it. "The certain piece of common ground," said Ben, "was that there is a broad subset of people who should not be armed, and right now, they are—and we could take legislative steps to address that. If we aren't trying to change it, we are contributing to it."

On my quest, I've met politicians on both sides of the aisle. As I often say, bullets do not know your political party and do not discriminate. Gun violence is not partisan, but the response to it often is. I am thankful for those who refuse to let this issue become partisan. One example for me is Governor Phil Murphy of New Jersey. It turned out he knew my cousin quite well. He got my number from her, and he called me in the days following Jaime's murder. He was a new governor at the time, and he promised me that he would make gun safety a focus of his, and boy, has he kept his word. In the weeks and months following our call, he used to regularly text me just to check in and make sure my family and I were okay. Despite being busy in his new role, he would regularly take time out to check in on my family.

It did not matter that we were not from New Jersey. People often ask me about politicians and tell me they are all the worst of the worst. I disagree. When I think about this, I am still amazed at the decency of people like Governor Murphy. What I have found is that politicians can be my helpers, and for me, the Governor is a helper.

A few months after Jaime's murder, he called me and shared his gun safety plan for New Jersey with me, then asked if I would be willing to come to the state to help him introduce it. Of course I said yes. I am so proud of what was accomplished as New Jersey passed some of the toughest gun safety laws in the nation. Through the leadership of Governor Murphy, they continue to do whatever they can to ensure the safety of New Jersey citizens.

Another example is the former governor of Ohio, John Kasich. People are often surprised when I say how much I like him and how much my conversation with him mattered to me. He is a conservative Republican from a conservative state, *and* he wanted to do something about gun violence. I spent a day with the guy when he asked me to testify in the Ohio State House about the success of the red flag law that we had passed in Florida. He is a really unique person with a lot of energy. He may be a conservative, but he is also very pragmatic. My family is in Cincinnati, Ohio, so my connections to the state run deep. My brother-in-law grew up there, and my sister raised her kids there. When I met with Kasich, he brought me to his office and said, "Tell me your story." I went right into it, and he was very engaged.

When I was done, he said, "So, do you believe in God?"

I told him the truth. I said, "At the moment, I haven't filed for a divorce between me and my religion, but I am kind of in a place where I'm ready to."

"I understand that," he said. "What religion?"

"Jewish," I said.

"Have you talked to your rabbi yet?" he asked.

"Yes."

"Well, keep talking," he said. "You'll find your way back."

I said, "I hope so. We'll see, but right now, I'm struggling."

I was being completely honest. I'd lost my belief in and connection to a higher power. When my brother was sick during his final illness, I was already struggling with this. At the hospice, the rabbi who would perform Michael's funeral came to us at his bedside and asked how we were doing. I told him how much I was struggling, given everything that Michael had done for people in his fifty years. We talked about "G-d's plan," and honestly, that gave me comfort and something that I could believe in. That was until my fourteen-year-old daughter was shot and killed.

Strangely, my faith is now stronger than ever. But rather than placing my faith in a higher power, I have faith directly and firmly in the people who surround me. While I often hear people talk about how miserably wretched others are, and say things like, "Politicians are the worst of the worst"—I experience the opposite every day.

I told John Kasich much of this, and our conversation around religion and the role that it can play continued for some time.

Kasich's staff explained what they needed from me in order to accomplish the work they were doing on red flag laws in Ohio. The meeting started, but it didn't seem like Kasich was listening; for a good five minutes, he scrolled on his phone. Then he paused the meeting and asked me to accompany him back to his office as he wanted me to look at something. That whole time in the meeting, he was looking for passages in scripture on his phone that he thought would give me comfort. He is a really unique guy, and he believes in gun safety! I was truly impressed by him. What was even more surprising was when I landed that night, I learned that he had taken time to call my wife to try and provide her with comfort as well.

One of the stranger encounters I've had as an activist happened at the Senate confirmation hearing for Supreme Court Associate Justice Brett Kavanaugh. Senator Dianne Feinstein invited me to the hearing as a guest. I had deep concerns over Justice Kavanaugh's confirmation as he had previously expressed antagonism to laws around gun safety.

The other guests and I were at the front of the room, in front of seated media and protesters. As I always did when I was in DC, I stood. I was in close proximity to Kavanaugh. It's hard to imagine he didn't notice me, as everyone else was seated.

As we took a break for lunch, I talked to Senator Blumenthal and then saw Kavanaugh a few feet from me. I moved forward to shake his hand, saying, "Hi, my name is Fred Guttenberg, father of Jaime Guttenberg, who was murdered in Parkland, Florida."

This is exactly how I introduce myself to everyone who might play a role in furthering this mission. My directness takes people aback, but most manage to transition to offering condolences. As soon as Kavanaugh heard me say, "murdered in Parkland," he quickly turned and walked away. White House Attorney Don McGahn, Deputy Attorney General Rod Rosenstein, and a security guy followed him.

At lunch I was bombarded with text messages regarding the attempted handshake. Apparently, reporters had captured the moment, and it rapidly went viral—then it was on fire. I was shocked by how quickly the news spread.

When I returned to the hearing room after lunch, I stood in my space again. Shortly after, Kavanaugh returned to the room, looked in my direction, and winked. I thought he was trying to use his gesture to suggest that all was okay, and I nodded back as if to say "no problem." I was wrong. Seconds later, three armed members of the Capitol Police removed me from the hearing room, only to interrogate me. They asked me to extend my right arm and to remove the three rubber bracelets I was wearing. These bracelets were imprinted with messages about my daughter. They asked the meaning of the bracelets, and I answered in a straightforward way. I also mentioned my mission and my purpose. I answered more questions, and then they asked for my license to do a background check. Upon completion of the background check, they returned my license to me, but two supervisors continued to interrogate me. Once they were convinced my intentions were harmless and that my only purpose had been to greet Kavanaugh and if possible, discuss gun safety, they allowed me to go back inside.

Once I returned to my seat, the security officer who had spent the morning with McGahn and Rosenstein now stood by my seat. He made it clear that I needed to sit for the rest of the day and that if I stood by my seat again as I had all morning, I would be removed. Since I wanted to stay, I sat down.

The thing about this entire encounter is what it taught me about activism. Simply put, not everyone is going to be a helper. I approached Justice Kavanaugh hoping to connect with him as two fathers from similar communities. His young daughters were also in the room. I had hoped that he would look into my eyes and think of every possible way to protect his children from what happened to my daughter while she was in school. Instead, I realized just how strong some people's antagonism to gun safety is, even when they are faced with the reality that it may one day impact their family.

In his written responses to the senators following the hearing, Kavanaugh wrote that he assumed the man who had approached him "and touched my arm" during a break at the Senate Judiciary Committee proceedings had been one of the many protesters in the hearing room.

"It had been a chaotic morning," Kavanaugh wrote. "I unfortunately did not realize that the man was the father of a shooting victim from Parkland, Florida. Mr. Guttenberg has suffered an incalculable loss. If I had known who he was, I would have shaken his hand, talked to him, and expressed my sympathy. And I would have listened to him." He had three days to do so but did not. In fact, once he found out who I was, his immediate response was to have me interrogated.

I consider his written response to have been dishonest. He knew the protesters were way back in the room and accompanied by watchful guards; they could not get anywhere close to him. On the second day, Senator Lindsey Graham asked Kavanaugh about his encounter with me, but Kavanaugh chose not to answer the question.

Since there was wide coverage of this hearing on both news and social media, if you wish, you can watch the publicly available video and decide for yourself.

Chapter 12

Father's Day

Orange Wave in November

Father's Day 2018 was going to be next to impossible for me to live through. I could not ignore it so I decided to flip it into something else. As part of my approach of mission and purpose going forward, I decided that Father's Day would have to stand for some greater meaning—not something to merely celebrate, but something that would remind fathers about protecting their kids. I went to all the dads I knew personally and on social media and suggested that instead of receiving cards and gifts and being pampered, we treat it as a day to show our wives and kids how much they are valued, and that we take the time to remember our roles as protectors and ultimately, to fight for gun safety.

I started an online challenge asking fathers to do crazy acts like an Ice Bucket Challenge using the color orange and then to post the video on social media with the hashtag #OrangeWaveInNovember. This was my way of getting dads to show that they care about gun safety and they vote. We have seen moms and kids step up and fight for their safety. I sincerely wanted to engage dads and encourage them to do more. I am not sure why dads overall are not fighting as hard as moms and kids. It is definitely something that bothers me, and I hope that my involvement and that of other involved dads will lead to a change.

Peter Yarrow of the group Peter, Paul and Mary rewrote "Puff the Magic Dragon" to incorporate the Orange Wave. Another dad did a skydive in orange. One father did an incredible rap song to the tune of Wyclef Jean's "Gone Till November." Musical acts became popular responses to the challenge. A local father who performs as a musician wrote an original song called, "Turn November Orange." The song begins with the words:

> For the love of my daughter,
> For the love of my son,
> Can't sit on the sidelines any longer,
> Something must be done.

His song "Turn November Orange" became a theme song for me through the election cycle.

There were so many original and memorable representations of this different take on Father's Day. I'd hoped to get a million participants, which was a bit of a reach. In actuality, I got thousands. But everywhere I went, I talked about the November election and gun safety. We kicked it off with a custom orange tarp over my pool that read, "Orange Wave in November." With drones flying overhead to capture video, I jumped into the pool to create a big splash and waves.

I wanted the election to turn on gun safety. We all know that after each election, voters are polled on which issues they considered most important or what drove their voting decision. Those who are elected track this information, and in some cases, have a mandate to pursue certain issues, especially when voters in overwhelming numbers say an issue is the highest priority to them. If incumbent officeholders want to be reelected, they need to be responsive on these issues or mandates. I wanted to make gun policy reform a mandate issue in that election and in all future elections, and I wanted to make it very clear to the winners that voters' desire for gun safety was part of why they won. We were successful enough to make a difference as voters in cities and states across the country reflected my own sentiments, creating an Orange Wave. We fired almost forty people in the House of Representatives, many of whom had the backing of the NRA. Gun safety will continue to be a mandate issue in elections going forward.

In the state of Florida, everyone thought the gun safety message lost in the last election; it did not. The only person who supported a strong statewide campaign on gun safety in Florida was Nikki Fried, who ran for the office of Commissioner of Agriculture and Consumer Services, the division that oversees background checks, permits, and licenses for guns. She won. The gun safety message was winning, even in pro-gun Florida. The gun lobby is losing.

Agriculture Commissioner Nikki Fried is the first woman elected to the position, the first Democrat to hold the position since 2001, and the only Democrat currently in statewide elected office in Florida. She is the first to say that Florida is...complicated. "Because our state is so different than other places in the country," she explained, "we've got three different states in one. You're always going to have those competing interests between urban and rural communities. Guns are a pivotal issue that divides those two communities."

What's amazing is the strong support Commissioner Fried received throughout the state, even in the rural areas where priorities on guns may be different than in population centers. That election gave me hope that even gun owners want gun safety. In fact, polling consistently shows that gun owners *do* want gun safety and that the only thing we need now is leaders willing to lead.

Commissioner Fried represents so much more than just promises, slogans, and prayers. Because of her time as a public defender, she has strong views on the connection between mental illness and gun violence. She sees gun violence as a patchwork of different problems to solve, and she discusses them in an intelligent, stern, and balanced way. "I can tell you that the vast majority of my repeat offenders had underlying mental health issues… We throw them into the prison system because we don't know what else to do with them. It's still a stigma to go to a counselor on school property, so I've been pushing for a law on mental health tele-visits so if someone needs counseling, they are not tied to hours in an office. It's still frowned upon. We still have issues with our veterans. Finally, we are recognizing that a significant population of veterans coming back from these overseas wars we've been in for close to twenty years have significant PTSD. We have to focus on these issues."

While traveling with Commissioner Fried and others running for office, I began to distinguish which of our elected officials cares deeply enough about the safety of our country to go beyond the podium—beyond the guest chair on the TV talk shows with the usual cup of coffee in front of them and the fake skyline behind them. I saw so many of them working tirelessly, not speaking superficially.

In my experience, Connecticut Senators Chris Murphy and Richard Blumenthal are among this group of upstanding people. Senator Murphy took office just before the Sandy Hook shooting, and then responded to that tragedy by declaring that his career would be defined by gun safety. His convictions are aligned with his direct experience.

Senator Murphy said, "My life was changed in an insignificant way compared to those directly affected by the Sandy Hook shooting. [But] I was given a mission that day: a mission to order my professional life in a way that sought to make sure that never happened again. I see a lot of signs that stain will remain. We have continued to build up a pretty massive political and social movement to make sure this rate of violence in America is unacceptable. For me, it is very personal. I was on site that day and saw and heard things I wish I could forget. But I also made friends in the following weeks and months with the families that mean more to me than anything."

Despite such intense efforts, I think there may have been a letdown effect in the wake of Sandy Hook—the mass murder of twenty children and six adults at an elementary school; people thought, *If Sandy Hook can't change the mind of Congress, nothing can.*

Senator Murphy's approach is evenhanded. "I understand how people think that," he said, "but it's not how politics work. There aren't epiphanies in American politics. There are the beginnings of movements. The shooting in 2012 marked the beginning of the anti-gun violence movement. Every single year since then, the gun lobby has gotten weaker. We still haven't made any significant breakthroughs federally, but we're winning more state legislation. We have more allies in Congress today than we did in 2012. We will have more support here to pass something meaningful." Right now, this country has decided to pour gasoline on the fire by sticking with some of the most loophole-ridden gun laws in the world. What we know is that background checks save lives. There are literally hundreds of thousands of people who have been denied access to a gun because they failed a background check. Not everybody who fails is going to commit acts of violence, but it stands to reason that if someone has committed serious violence in the past or has a serious mental illness, they shouldn't own a gun.

The background check system doesn't apply to as many sales as it should, but a lot of people who shouldn't own firearms are stopped from buying weapons. The problem is it only applies to guns, not ammunition. You need both guns and ammunition to take a life. It stands to reason that you should hold ammunition transactions to the same standards that we apply to purchases of the weapon itself. If we did that, not a single law-abiding responsible citizen would be denied the ability to buy bullets for their gun, but the same set of people who shouldn't own guns are probably the same set of people who shouldn't own ammunition."

It is both fascinating and alarming to reflect on gun use through the years and observe how what's occurring today may be a kind of societal breakdown in America. Is it a societal breakdown? Is it the reality of what happens when you continue to weaken gun laws? Is it both? How much innocent blood has to be spilled? Everyone deserves security. And I damned sure know that our kids should be safe in schools and other environments away from home. The thought of how these people in power are either contributing to our safety or harm is dizzying. Ultimately, we don't have much control of our own well-being as it relates to a stranger's gun, ammunition, intentions, mental state, and callous lack of empathy. We also cannot rely on the idea that it won't happen to us.

I really applaud Commissioner Fried, as well as the Senators and the House members who want to do something for asking poignant questions that matter, every day. Their convictions and their support for the gun safety movement keep me going, particularly on tough days when I just want to hug my daughter and hear her laughter. Commissioner Fried is certainly one with whom I've shared hugs, laughter, and tears.

Of our friendship and alliance, she states: "Fred makes me cry every time he talks. He spoke at my transition and inauguration. He says that I remind him of his daughter, which always makes me cry. What Fred has been able to do is take his pain and his loss and put it toward smart advocacy. If you see what he tweets and says, there is thought behind it—and heart. He's not just railing against the system—he's on a mission to make a change. I commend him for taking a horrific event in his life and doing something good with that. When I make comments, and as I try to make policies inside my office, I definitely have Fred sitting on my shoulder."

Chapter 13

State of My Union

Being removed from the 2020 State of the Union

She's been called "Public Enemy No. 1" by teachers and education professionals across the country. Secretary of Education Betsy DeVos has never worked in education, though Congress confirmed her by a narrow margin.

Her failure could not have been more clearly shown than it was by her response to the shooting at MSD. She was asked by the President to do a report on the Parkland shooting. When she announced this and explained that they would look at everything *but* the role of guns, it was obvious this report was bound to be troublesome. How could you look at this instance of gun violence and not consider the role of guns in gun violence? Or even factors such as age of ownership or safe storage?

When the report was due to be released, the White House invited the families of the Parkland shooting to come for a private briefing. The President was to be in attendance, as were his daughter Ivanka and his son-in-law Jared Kushner. I have no need to meet with the President for any other reason but for him to do something about gun violence. I didn't need the photo opportunity, and I also did not need to be a part of the *President's* photo opportunity. At any other time, it would have been amazing to go to visit the White House and the Oval Office, but I had to stand by my convictions. Because I considered this report a failure due to its inability to address the *guns* in gun violence, I refused to go.

Two days after the meeting, I got a call from another father who did go to the White House meeting. He had just received a call from the White House wanting to know why I wasn't there and asking if I would be willing to speak to them.

I casually said, "We can set something up."

"Now," he said. "They're on the phone now."

The representative on the phone was Theo Wold, the special assistant to the President's Domestic Policy Council. With regards to domestic policy, he is very close to the President. Theo wanted to know why I felt it would have been a mistake to attend. So I told him. He was very nice, and he said he "understood."

He said, "What if I told you that I may be more aligned with things you want to do than you would think?"

I replied, "What does that mean? On gun policy? Knowing who you work for, I'm not sure I would believe that."

Taking a breath, he said, "That's fair, but I am, and I have the President's ear. I would like to meet with you."

With that, I turned up my volume a bit, firmly stating, "The first thing you can do is get your boss to stop calling people like me who are working to reduce gun violence 'haters of the Second Amendment' and 'gun grabbers.' It is not true, and those comments incite violence."

He said, "I can work on that."

A few days later, it became clear that the White House was upset with the feedback on the DeVos report; it did not get the reaction that they had hoped it would. They were clearly upset at the limited attention it received and that most of the attention it did garner was negative. The media did not ignore the report's neglect of the gun issue. Apparently, the communications team wanted to attack those of us advocating for gun safety, but Theo claimed he had put a stop to that. Again, I just want to reiterate that this report on gun violence did not examine *guns*. DeVos aspired to allocate federal funding for the use of firearms and firearms training in schools. Her stance: Addressing gun violence in schools doesn't involve gun safety measures.

Following my second conversation with Theo, in which we discussed his efforts to manage the White House reply to the DeVos report, I decided to meet with him in DC. This meeting was going to be on White House grounds in the Executive Building. We did not announce it, and it did not include media.

The day I was supposed to meet with Theo, the government shutdown began. The meeting did not happen until three months later, when we spent about ninety minutes discussing what my ideally preferred approach to gun safety would be. We discussed background checks, Centers for Disease Control funding, repeal of the Protection of Lawful Commerce in Arms Act (PLCCA), raising the minimum age to purchase guns to twenty-one, safe storage of weapons, 3D printed weapons, Extreme Risk Protection Orders aka red flag laws, high-capacity magazines, and other public policy specifics. My hope was that we would continue the conversation, but I never heard from Theo again.

While I am disappointed in the inability of this White House to do anything of substance about gun violence, the reality is that every single day since Jaime's murder has brought something or someone special to further my mission.

One of those people is Speaker of the House Nancy Pelosi. While we had met previously, on July 24, 2018, she and Congressman Ted Deutch invited me to tell my story to the House Minority Caucus. I did so and talked about the coming challenge of 3D printed firearms, but I also ended up veering away from my prepared remarks and challenging the caucus very sternly. I told them I thought they were failing on this issue and why. I was certainly tougher than I had planned to be, but I'm appreciative that the Speaker gave me the chance to address them and thankful that my message was understood.

She tells me she remembers it well. "When we knew you were coming, it was a humbling anticipation. We knew you would challenge our conscience to do something, but you also challenged our knowledge on other possibilities [such as] the 3D printed gun legislation, which most of us in the room didn't have a full knowledge of, along with the urgency. So for us in the room, challenging of conscience is what we are here for.

"You were absolutely right, and as you know, that was very close to the time [of the shooting], so you [had] the courage and perseverance to channel your grief into an energy to help save other lives and to be so passionate in terms of knowledge about the issues at hand and how we should go forward. That is what you demonstrated in the room that day."

For me to be able to address that caucus was huge, but to have a meaningful impact on them is a moment I will never forget. When I remember the reaction we had together afterwards, I'm just thankful.

It gave me great hope when Speaker Pelosi decided to make gun safety and victims of gun violence a central focus at the 2019 State of the Union address, to which she invited me as her guest for the first time. While the House of Representatives and the Speaker highlighted the issue of gun violence with their choices of guests and the work that they were doing to reduce gun violence, the same could not be said of our President. Sadly, he mostly ignored the issue—only calling it out as a reason why he says we need a southern border wall.

When I left the 2019 State of the Union speech, rather than feeling in awe of the moment, I was so angry with the President that I went back to my hotel and wrote the following opinion piece about his failure on this issue, an op-ed which was published in *Newsweek* the next day.

I Was at Trump's State of the Union. I Shouldn't Have Been.

Several days ago I was invited by Speaker Pelosi to attend the State of the Union as her guest. She is arguably the second most powerful person in the country. While I should have felt good and as if this was an amazing moment, I did not. I should

not have been there. I should have been home
watching on our couch with my complete family.

I cannot erase the reality that I was there because
my daughter was murdered.

I was honored to be a guest of our Speaker, and
the fact that so many victims of gun violence
were there too made me feel optimistic that gun
safety would be front and center at the State of
the Union. Victims of gun violence from across
the country were present. From Parkland alone,
besides myself, Charlie Mirsky of March For Our
Lives was also invited by the Speaker; Manny
Oliver, whose son Joaquin was killed, was invited
by Congressman Deutch; activist and MSD
student survivor Cameron Kasky was invited by
Congressman Swalwell; and Andrew Pollack,
whose daughter, Meadow, was killed, was invited
by Senator Scott.

There were other victims from across the country.
Victims were invited by Representatives and
Senators, Democrats and Republicans. My hope
was that this speech would recognize the true
national emergency on gun violence and recognize
that it is a bipartisan emergency that affects both
Republicans and Democrats. My hope was that
this speech would provide a road map on how to
deal with the reality of gun violence. Wow, was
I disappointed.

Our President last night hit on several topics, but
the one that stood out for me was his made-up
version of an emergency. His recitation of facts

on undocumented immigrants and a crisis on
our southern border was simply too much for
me to take.

We do have a real crisis in this country, a real
emergency. In the United States of America,
over 40,000 people now die every year from gun
violence. That is a higher rate of death than from
traffic accidents. The President refused to discuss
that reality.

As the President knew during his speech, on the
following day, the first hearings in over eight years
on gun violence prevention would be held by
the House Judiciary committee. He could have
mentioned that, along with his hope to work with
legislators on gun violence. He stayed silent. He
stayed irrelevant. He chose to not be useful on
this real emergency. He chose to focus on an issue
that ignites his base and to ignore the rest of the
country who deal with the reality of gun violence
every day.

While watching this speech, sadly, I realized that
had my daughter's killer been an illegal immigrant,
the President would have mentioned it. He failed
to mention it because like so many victims of gun
violence, she was killed by an American male.
Even when the President mentioned the heroism
of the Pittsburgh survivors, he failed to mention
the fact that a gun, an AR-15 which made its way
into a temple, was used to massacre people in that
temple. Why doesn't President Trump consider
40,000 people dying a national emergency?

> It is sad to realize that if all gun violence were only
> committed by illegal aliens, this President would
> be working overtime to do something about it.

Speaker Pelosi did not give up on efforts to highlight gun safety,
and she invited me to be her guest again at the 2020 State of the
Union. As I explained in this book's introduction, my emotions
started to get to me when Trump talked about the violent threat
of illegal immigrants. He was blaming violence on them, and that
was inaccurate. I wanted to yell out that the person who killed
my daughter was an American, not an immigrant. Later on in the
speech, he started with the nonsense that he was going to protect
the Second Amendment, using his bully pulpit as a megaphone
for the NRA; when he said that across the country the Second
Amendment was under attack, and every Republican jumped up
like a bunch of well-trained animals and started to cheer, I lost it.
I had been quiet all night, but at that, I stood up and yelled back,
saying only nine words: "What about victims of gun violence like
my daughter?"

Within seconds, I was confronted by security. As I walked out of
the chamber, I thought that I would simply be asked to leave, but
that's not what happened. My outburst got me handcuffed and
detained by the Capitol Police. Following some questioning, I
was walked to the garage below, still in handcuffs, and questioned
again. The questions were very basic. They wanted to know if
I was part of a planned protest. They wanted to know if I had
anything else I planned to do. They wanted to know why I
made my outburst. They said that I was going to be arrested. I
asked if I would need an attorney, and they said no. I asked if
I could borrow a phone to call my wife as mine was in Speaker
Pelosi's office, and they said no. All of my personal items were
removed and placed in a bag. I was then placed with my hands

still handcuffed behind my back in a vehicle that was essentially a small metal box with no windows.

I was scared—I had no idea where they were transporting me. Fortunately, the drive was only to a detention facility about five minutes away. The police put me in a holding room with my left arm handcuffed to a wall. I was told I would be there most of the night, as I was under arrest. I was never actually clear on the charge, and when I again asked if I needed an attorney, I was told no. I was also never read my Miranda rights.

Thankfully, at some point shortly after the speech ended, Speaker Pelosi and Congressman Ted Deutch intervened and spoke with the Capitol Police, and I was released sometime after that. Surprised, I asked if there was a place where I could walk to grab a cab to my hotel, but they told me someone was already waiting for me. When I walked to the front of the detention facility to retrieve my personal belongings, two members of Speaker Pelosi's staff were waiting to drive me back to my hotel.

As I mentioned earlier, I was upset and apologetic when the Speaker called, but she could not have been more gracious and told me I did not owe her an apology. She told me that she understood how hard it had to have been for me to listen to that speech and that I spoke for America. She then let me know that she had heard enough of that speech and had ripped up her copy of the State of the Union address. I hadn't known this, as I had been removed before it happened. I felt I was the one who'd screwed up, yet Speaker Pelosi was helping *me* to feel better. On a night when I desperately needed it, she was my helper.

My wife and son were livid with me—and justifiably so. They hadn't watched the State of the Union because they knew how this President would speak about the violence that impacted our family. They didn't know what had happened to me until friends and family members started texting and calling to see if I was okay. They couldn't get in touch with me because my phone was still in Speaker Pelosi's office. I had put my family in the same place Jaime's shooter had put us in—the not knowing part—and I felt terrible for it. For my family, this was a triggering event. The last time we could not reach someone on a cell phone, it was my daughter on the day that she was murdered.

I was still very upset when I went to sleep that night. I'd let my grief and emotions get the best of me. But I felt much better the next day when I saw how this nation was discussing gun safety because of what had happened, and even rallying to support what I did. One of the top trending hashtags on Twitter that day was #IStandWithFred. Perhaps this is what Speaker Pelosi meant when she spoke to me for my book. "One of the most important things that I have said to our members or advocates is to believe," she told me; "*Believe*. You have to believe that you can change minds. We have to believe when we're listening to you about the credibility and authenticity of your argument. It's no use to just be in the room. It has to be about belief."

Speaker Pelosi then went on to say, "Fred, this is how I would describe you: I believe that faith gives people hope. Sometimes people are rallying for something, and they're being negative. I say, don't be negative, because if you are taking the time to change minds, you wouldn't be here if you didn't think you could change their minds! Your strength, your persistence, which I'm sure you had before, is greatly enhanced by the tragedies your family faced, so thank you for believing you could make a difference and instilling belief in the rest of us that gives us hope. ...You believe something can happen because of the charity that you hope people have in their hearts to come to the right conclusion."

Just before telling me this, Speaker Pelosi had left a press conference discussing the passage of the 9/11 Compensation Bill. She had a chance to work on this with other true American heroes, such as John Feal and Jon Stewart, who committed their lives to being helpers to those still affected by 9/11, and who had spent the prior months giving impassioned testimony and putting a spotlight on the rampant illness and death among first responders at the World Trade Center.

It is astonishing how on this day, the loss of my daughter and the loss of my brother would converge in this conversation.

At the end of our call, she said, "As a mother of five children and nine grandchildren, I can't even imagine the courage it takes to do what you do, but thank you for turning that grief into safety for other people."

For such a respected figure as Speaker of the House Pelosi, the first woman in history to hold this high office, to tell me how courageous I am continues to mystify me, which is the only reason I'm sharing it. These moments that have defined my advocacy give me hope. Speaker Pelosi is a helper. I never thought of the people who surround me as helpers until after Jaime died. Now that I understand that we all have our helpers; we only need to be willing to look for them and accept the help.

What I couldn't get as far as much needed action from either the White House or the Senate, I gained twofold in corporate solidarity. I've been aggressive and haven't given the gun lobby an inch. In the days following Jaime's murder and since then, I have spoken about "going after their money." The first big crack in the gun lobby's armor was at Dick's Sporting Goods; they decided they would stop selling certain weapons and would no longer sell to anyone under the age of twenty-one. Previously, business and political leaders had been afraid to make decisions that would go against the wishes of the NRA. This decision by Dick's changed that. Walmart decided to do the same thing the following day.

The connection between what happened in Parkland and Dick's Sporting Goods runs deeper than most people know. A friend of mine from my Dunkin' Donuts days was vice president of marketing at Dick's at the time Jaime was killed. This gave Dick's a personal connection to Parkland. Because of this connection and the steps taken by Dick's following the shooting, I arranged for their CEO, Ed Stack, and his executive team to come visit my family and the other Parkland families about a month after the shooting. This was done without publicity at the time, but it has since been made public.

When Ed Stack spoke to us, he discussed the changes that the company had already made in the days following the Parkland shooting around the retailing of guns in his stores, reaffirming that they would look for other ways to both go further and to lead on this issue, both in the business world and politically. For me, Ed Stack is not only a helper, he is a hero. He was the first to show that a business could go against the gun lobby and not only do okay, but thrive. He has never wavered, and to this day, his company continues to lead.

The approach of the first Mother's Day since the shooting was emotional for my wife and for the sixteen other moms and wives who lost loved ones in the Parkland shooting. Though they knew that this was a day they would not be celebrating, they were filled with appreciation for what Dick's had done, so they turned Mother's Day into a day with a purpose. Following the meeting with Dick's, they decided to organize a national shop-in over Mother's Day weekend at Dick's Sporting Goods and Walmart to thank them for the steps they had taken. They coordinated an online campaign to encourage people to go shop at Dick's or

Walmart on Mother's Day as a show of appreciation, which drew some media attention as well. They all coordinated their own shopping events locally to highlight the campaign and share it on social media and via traditional media. They channeled their grief into the mission that weekend in a very meaningful way.

The decision by Dick's Sporting Goods to exit the gun business was a key factor in weakening the NRA. Other conversations in the corporate world picked up momentum. We have seen multiple retailers making changes to their policies as well, and banks such as Citibank and Bank of America have also parted ways with the gun business.

Every setback for the NRA was like spotting a crack in the NRA's armor. They no longer seemed invincible. And every one of these cracks revealed how more and more people could go against this powerful gun lobby and not pay a price, and each showed how success begets success so long as you stay the course.

My fight for Jaime and to reduce gun violence led me to Jaime's Law. Congresswoman Debbie Wasserman-Schultz and Senator Richard Blumenthal introduced the Ammunition Background Check, also known as "Jaime's Law." Knowing my daughter's name is embedded in a proposed federal law is kind of surreal. It's a source of sadness and pride: pride in the slight justice from her death that it symbolizes, and in its intent to save lives.

Congresswoman Wasserman-Schultz had fought for gun safety for many years before we met on the night of the vigil for Parkland victims.

As she said then, "Gun violence is clearly a public health crisis, and it is really time for our country to approach it as such... [W]hen we were looking into the various ways we could address the scourge of gun violence. there were a lot of members who had introduced gun safety-related legislation, but they focused on the weapon. I had not previously known that just like guns themselves, which are prohibited from being purchased by people who are adjudicated mentally ill, ammunition is also prohibited under federal law from being purchased by those people in the same categories. Yet there are no background checks at all. When I learned that, I said, 'Oh my gosh, we have to introduce legislation to address this.' I introduced the Ammunition Background Check Act, [but] Republicans, who were in the majority, had no interest in moving anything meaningful [forward] when it came to addressing gun safety. It went nowhere."

Just before the 2018 election, I met with Congresswoman Wasserman Schultz to discuss my concern about the approximately 400 million weapons already on the street today and the challenge of doing anything about them. She told me about the previous effort to pass background checks on ammunition as a way to address this issue. I asked her if she would be willing to try again, and during this conversation, we discussed renaming it Jaime's Law. We will pass this law, and I firmly believe that Jaime will save lives through this law.

"At the end of the day…without the ammunition, the gun is not deadly or harmful," Congresswoman Wasserman Schultz insisted. "The fact that a felon can walk into a retail store and walk out with hundreds of rounds of ammunition without so much as leaving their name is unconscionable. …The message of more guns in more public places is not the answer to violence," she said. "There is a reason other countries have a rate of only .1 per 100,000 people for gun deaths. Ours is 4.4 per 100,000 people. That is forty-four times higher than similar countries. The difference is [that they have] stronger gun safety laws in countries like Japan, China, UK, and South Korea. The facts are

staring us right in the face. When you spend your first half of
your life as a legislator, you delight in incremental change. You
learn that you're pushing a boulder up a steep hill, and sometimes
you're going to roll back a few steps. You have to stand up for
what's right. You have to steel your spine and keep fighting.
Know that one person can make a difference. You have to be
willing to recognize that the wheels of progress turn slowly. Any
little bit of progress you make in preventing gun violence actually
saves lives."

I have been touched by learning the personal stories of those who
have fought at my side. To reiterate Alyssa Milano's point about
gaining consensus on tough matters, when you overlay a human
story onto policy and procedure, change becomes dynamic, even
electric, as it is built by people. There are many examples, but
to highlight just a few, I am amazed by my friend Dr. Joseph
Sakaran, who was a teenage victim of gun violence, as he was
once shot in the neck, but he then went on to become a trauma
surgeon helping victims of gun violence. My friends Mike and
Kristin Song lost their son Ethan around the same time we lost
Jaime. He went to a friend's house to play, a gun was left out in
the house by the parent, and Ethan was killed. They have since
gone on to fight for safe storage laws in Connecticut, where
this happened, and around the country. My friends Lonnie and
Sandy Phillips lost their daughter in the movie theater shooting in
Aurora, Colorado, and now spend their life traveling the country
to help victims of gun violence who are in need of support. There
is Shaundelle Bess Brooks, whose son was murdered in the Waffle
House shooting in Nashville, Tennessee; she has been fighting
for change there. And closer to home, there are the sixteen other
families who along with me lost children or spouses on that tragic
day in Parkland. We do not all agree on solutions, but we are
all fighting to make our schools and America a safer place. With

40,000 victims of gun violence every year, examples of stories like these exist all over America. Together, we are going to solve this problem.

Congressman Eric Swalwell is a former prosecutor whose father is a retired police officer and whose two younger brothers currently serve in law enforcement. He was in orientation as a newly elected congressman when the Sandy Hook shooting occurred. He is also a young father. We had common ground and sort of a brotherly bond that encouraged me to travel with him during his run for president.

About a month before he announced his run for the presidency, he alerted me that he would be doing so and that gun safety would be his core message. He wanted to kick off his campaign in Parkland and enlisted my help. While we also discussed the idea of an endorsement, I insisted that I would not make any endorsements for candidates—I wanted to keep my focus on the issue of gun safety and hear from all of the candidates on the matter. What I *did* endorse was the idea of building a campaign around the issue of gun safety, and I will be forever grateful that Congressman Swalwell did this.

The day after he announced his candidacy on *The Late Show with Steven Colbert*, Congressman Swalwell came to Parkland. I had helped to plan and organize the event and had suggested and then helped to secure the location. He asked if I would be part of his rally and speak after him. Of course, I agreed.

Before the rally, we met up and drove together to the school where my daughter was murdered. He wanted to see the location for himself. We then drove to a temporary memorial in Coral Springs—a wooden temple built by a nationally known artist. The temple was designed so that people could place mementos or memories of those who had died there. The plan was to burn the temple and everything inside of it a few months later as a way of letting go.

Congressman Swalwell wanted to visit this memorial and leave a message. It was a very emotional moment for the Congressman as he was surrounded by the reality of what had been lost, there amidst the memories and mementos of those who had been killed.

Next, we headed to the rally. The truth is, I had never been part of something like this before, and I did not go with a written speech. I often prefer speaking without written notes, so I decided to wing it. But my wife was concerned, considering that I was attending a kickoff event for a potential future President, and tried to get me to write a speech. I thought about it but wasn't sure what I wanted to write. I was waiting for some kind of inspiration.

Before the rally, I watched Congressman Swalwell and his wife holding their baby daughter and interacting with her. I had my inspiration. I started my speech by talking about memories of holding my baby daughter; I described the day we brought her home from the hospital, and then I talked about the day we buried her because of gun violence. I spoke about watching her grow up through the age of fourteen and the reality that I will not be able to watch her get any older because of gun violence. I then thanked Congressman Swalwell for running; I grabbed his arm and let him know that he had just catapulted gun safety into the Presidential election. The fact is that because of Congressman Swalwell, gun safety became an issue that every candidate was forced to discuss. I will be forever grateful to him for courageously doing this and for our ongoing friendship.

I truly believed that he would make a fantastic US President, and it had not escaped me that he had participated in the

Congressional sit-in for gun safety in 2016 for twenty-six hours. When I asked him if his position had changed as he traveled the country, he said, "What I've come to find is that it's not an issue to be afraid of. I thought that I would feel so much resistance and the real world would feel like Twitter, with more haters than people supporting you, since this is a hot burner issue. But it's not. In the number of places I've been inside the country, Midwest, Southeast, up and down the coast, I thought I would run into more people saying provocative things to me about me trying to take their guns away. But people overwhelmingly say, 'Thank you for caring about this issue.' What it shows me is that the 'resistance' to common sense gun safety legislation is just a vocal [but] tiny minority."

I'm exceptionally proud to say that together, we made the issue of gun violence a top-tier issue in the 2020 election. After he offered a plan, other candidates proactively came forward with their own plans for gun safety. According to Congressman Swalwell, it had never been an issue on which candidates would lead; previously, it had remained more of a reactive Q & A issue for most candidates.

"We have the best opportunity to negotiate *up* now on gun safety, whereas we've always negotiated down," he said. "My coming to Congress moment was Sandy Hook. I was in Congressional orientation when Sandy Hook happened. As awful as it was, I thought, *This is an opportunity where we can actually do something about what just happened.* We sought background checks, and the NRA and Republicans said no, and it failed. After more and more shootings, possibly [after] Orlando, we sought to say that if you are on a terrorist watch list, you couldn't buy a gun. All of a sudden, the Republicans who wrote laws and carried out practices that discriminated against Muslim Americans in the days and weeks after September 11 to make sure that we were safe had no problem doing that. All of a sudden, they were the biggest defenders of making sure that no one [who was] accidentally placed on the terrorist watch list could be barred from buying a gun. That is how far they were willing to go to keep us from doing anything. Then after Vegas, we had a crazy idea that maybe that device that turned a semiautomatic assault rifle into a fully automatic rifle, the bump stock, should be banned. They wouldn't even go for that. We were just continuing to negotiate down.

"After Parkland, the way [the students] organized and marched, we all had their back and community groups came together. We beat seventeen NRA-endorsed members of Congress. The message I take from that is we have momentum. Yes, background checks [are important], but that should be the floor, not the ceiling."

Over the course of his presidential run, I joined Congressman Swalwell at numerous events, including the introduction of his comprehensive gun safety plan. His location for the unveiling: in front of the NRA headquarters in Virginia. Needless to say, I couldn't miss that one. Congressman Swalwell invited me as his guest for the night of the first presidential debate in Miami. I sat in the front row with his wife, who excitedly pointed, indicating the tie he was wearing. It was orange, to honor Jaime and the other victims of gun violence. In addition, he was wearing the orange ribbon that I had given to him on his suit. What I remember about that night was how nervous she was and how she grabbed my arm all night, worried about how he was doing. We were both extremely proud of him and thought he did great.

I kept waiting for the moderators to ask questions about gun violence, but it was not happening. Midway through the debate, NBC changed moderators; now Chuck Todd and Rachel Maddow were up. But again, they did not ask questions regarding

this issue; so by the time of the first commercial break, I had
simply had enough. I got out of my seat and started marching
over to yell at them to ask a question about gun violence. I hadn't
gotten far when I felt two sets of arms grabbing me and pulling
me back: security. I guess I was not supposed to do that. I tried
to explain what my intention was, and thankfully, Congressman
Swalwell saw the commotion and came over to see what was
going on. He informed them that I was his guest and they asked
me to return to my seat.

The debate continued and later on, the moderators did finally
ask a question on gun violence. A few months later, after his
presidential campaign had ended, Congressman Swalwell was
asked in an interview about his favorite moments from the
campaign, and he spoke about this moment as one of the ones
he will remember most, as it showed him how every day, people
fight for what matters most to them. He said he will always
remember the image of me getting pulled back because of how
determined I was to get them to ask questions on gun violence.
I am eternally grateful to Congressman Swalwell for focusing
his campaign on gun safety. While this campaign cycle ended
for him, I am certain that his presence on our national stage will
continue to grow.

After the debate, as everyone in the audience was now up and
strolling around, I walked across the debate floor and saw Vice
President Joe Biden standing on the stage talking to another
candidate. He saw me looking over in his direction and waved for
me to come towards the stage.

Amazingly, he crouched down on one knee and grabbed my
hand. Photographers captured the moment, but what the
photographers did not capture was our conversation. He
remembered me from our earlier meeting over a year prior, only

a few weeks after Jaime was murdered. More astonishingly, he remembered what he had spoken to me about and he remembered my wife and my son. He asked how things were going with regards to the advice that he'd given me and wanted to know how my wife and son were doing. I was truly blown away. Vice President Biden had just finished an intense debate, and now he was engaging me in conversation in a way that was so focused and so personal, it was as if the debate had not even happened.

I often recall how people who I never expected to know have come into my life and given me hope; this moment gives me hope.

I was regularly asked if I planned to endorse Vice President Joe Biden for president, but I always stuck to my belief that I didn't have a need to endorse anyone yet. I wanted to hear all of the candidates discussing gun safety and elevating the issue.

I had written about my heartfelt encounters with Biden on Twitter; then a few months after the debate, the Biden campaign asked if I would share them in a commercial. I agreed on the condition that they were not expecting an endorsement. It is a testament to Vice President Biden and his campaign that they didn't push me, but wanted to share the story as part of their focus on gun safety. I was happy to do that.

My decision to endorse Vice President Biden was sudden and impulsive. The night of the South Carolina primary, Jen and I were at a friend's house, sitting around a campfire and talking about the primary results. My friends asked me what I thought would happen with the rest of the campaign. "It's a huge win for Biden, obviously," I said. "I think it'll change the direction of the campaign." I also said that I now felt that Biden could and would win the nomination and be the candidate to challenge Trump. Not only was he committed to doing something about gun violence, he was now also in the best position as a candidate to do so. I said to my friends that night that it was time to endorse him.

My wife and my friends challenged me, since I'd insisted earlier that it was important to wait. But I felt good about the decision, it was the right time, and I haven't looked back since. The following morning, I went on Twitter and Facebook and wrote out my endorsement:

"Last night, I decided that the time has come for me to make a decision in the Presidential primary as my vote in Florida is only two weeks away. I have decided to endorse Joe Biden for President. He again showed this country that he is a fighter for us, a fighter who understands how to fight and win, but also how to fight with decency, integrity, civility, and honor. Those are the qualities needed to defeat the current occupant of the White House and to restore America following [his departure].

Anyone who has followed my story knows just how much the Vice President has meant to me and my process of healing. That said, I waited this long because of how much I like many of the other candidates and how much I believed some of them could also have been great presidents and may one day be great presidents. For me, it came down to this. I believe this election is not only about the next president, but it is also about flipping the Senate, firing McConnell, and holding the House. I believe Vice President Biden can *win* and do this and be the right person for our times. I believe we can trust him. I believe we can count on him to put America and our interests above his own. My dream of getting true gun safety done requires all of this. I look forward to doing anything the Vice President needs to ensure his election, flip the Senate, and hold the House. I then look forward to working with him to pass gun safety measures that will lead to a reduction in the gun violence death rate in America.

My endorsement for Vice President Biden is done with complete and total respect for the other candidates. I personally have met and spoken with Mayor Bloomberg and am so thankful for everything he has done to fight for gun safety and for America. I personally have met with Mayor Pete Buttigieg and think his future as a leader in America is here, and I look forward to seeing the amazing things he will do. I am thankful for Amy Klobuchar and Elizabeth Warren and the commitments that they have made to fighting gun violence. I am thankful for the issues highlighted by Tom Steyer and his graceful exit last night and his commitment to defeating the current occupant of the White House. That said, the time for this country to unite behind a candidate to defeat the current occupant of the White House and flip the Senate is *now*!

I hope that these other candidates agree with my position and quickly make decisions to support Vice President Biden, or as I will be calling him from now on, the next President of the United States of America. It is time for us to look forward and to restore the fabric of our amazing country. Joe Biden is the person to do this, and it is my honor to offer my full endorsement. A few months ago, I did this commercial for the VP, long before I was ready to endorse [anyone]. I did so because of my belief in him as a person and what he meant to my healing. I hope you will watch this now!"

As part of this endorsement, I shared the commercial from months earlier on social media. I had not alerted the campaign to my decision in advance, so everyone saw it for the first time on Twitter and Facebook. While it took me a long time to get to this decision, I am thrilled to have the chance to support a person as decent as Joe Biden and to work to make him our next President.

I know with certainty that Joe Biden as President will ensure that this country finally has true gun safety in place.

Chapter 14

It Could Be You

Pursuing my mission

On Valentine's Day of 2018, the only other parent I personally knew who also suffered a loss that day was Max Schachter. His son, Alex, was also killed in the Parkland shooting. Max's brother-in-law was my business partner, who I've known for a long time. The idea that we both lost children on this day, in this way, is insane. I hate that I know any of the parents that way. As I always tell them, "I hate that I know you, but I love you."

Amongst the 17 families who lost loved ones, we do get together as a group of families. While we may not all agree on how to solve the issues that brought us together, we will always share this bond because of who we lost. Getting together has been therapeutic for us. When you're with people who have gone through something

like this with you, you can have conversations that you may
not be able to have with others. It provides us with a strange
sense of normalcy, since they understand how you feel and you
understand how they feel. People who do not share the bond of
such an experience with you may not understand as deeply.

As for my family, we are different. We are learning as we go.
The first summer following the murder, we decided to go on
our first vacation together. It almost didn't happen. We planned
a road trip with our dogs, but then five minutes into the drive
Jesse didn't want to go. He felt this was not a "family" vacation
without Jaime.

"This isn't right," he said. "She's not in the seat next to me."

He got upset and my wife got emotional. They both wanted
to turn around. I refused. I felt terrible forcing the issue by not
turning around, but I also felt we needed to do this. While this
was not our family the way it used to be, we were still a family,
and we needed to get through a first family vacation together. We
continued on our drive to the Georgia mountains. As this was the
first vacation that we ever took with our dogs, they turned out
to be our helpers this week as they made this vacation different
and gave us comfort. While the week was not great, we did get
through our first vacation together following our loss of Jaime,
and we have gone on others since.

And so we go on, finding more helpers all the while, like my
friend Po Murray. Her four children went to Sandy Hook,
and her youngest was in the sixth grade at the intermediate
school when the tragedy occurred. Of all the people she could
have lived next door to, the shooter was her neighbor. As she
explains, "We lost children and educators we knew because
we were in that school for over twelve years. On that Friday,
I made a commitment to do something about this. I couldn't

believe that assault weapons were available and that there were not universal background checks. I took it for granted we had a system of checks and balances and strong laws to protect our kids. I had no idea until that tragedy occurred. I decided to form the Newtown Alliance."

"The tragedy that occurred in Parkland," Po said, "hit us really hard in Newtown because the similarities between the two tragedies were uncanny. We watched those students walk out of the building the way that the Sandy Hook children did, hands on each other's shoulders. It brought back horrific memories."

The question on everyone's mind is, what are the keys to gaining consensus in the arena of gun safety? We have many national organizations and state organizations working on this issue, though not necessarily in a coordinated fashion. Right from the get-go, Po recognized this, and she decided that Newtown Alliance, where I now serve on the board, needed to initiate campaigns and strategies to pull everyone together. They decided to hold a national vigil for all victims of gun violence to elevate families and survivors of gun violence and to honor the lives lost not only in Sandy Hook but elsewhere. They pulled all the groups together to be unified in messaging for at least the month of December, the anniversary of Sandy Hook.

I also met people such as Congresswoman Debbie Mucarsel-Powell in Florida, who lost her father to gun violence, and Congresswoman Lucy McBath in Georgia, who lost her son to gun violence. Both were inspired to action, ran for Congress, and won in 2018. Then there was Congressman Mike Levin in San Diego, California, who ran and won in 2018 and made gun safety a core focus of his platform.

"The only conclusion is that we put people in charge who will do something to pre-empt future tragedies," Congressman Levin said. "What that means is we have leadership that is not only looking at background checks and closing loopholes, but also trying to put an assault weapons ban [into effect], trying to make sure we ban bump stocks, and we also need to fund research into gun violence from CDC. They have a mandate to do the research, but there is no money [for it], which is absurd. We need to cut out the talk of concealed [carry permit] reciprocity. The NRA wants to make it the law of the land, so the gun laws of West Virginia will all of a sudden become the gun laws of San Diego. I don't think that is what anyone wants to see.

"We have a lot more to do. We can't go through this routine anymore. We've got to stand up to the NRA and do all we can to fight for the broader public. I would say the NRA does not represent the interests of most gun owners. They represent the narrow interests of a handful of gun manufacturers. I would like to believe manufacturers would be open to suggestions to keep their products out of the hands of people who shouldn't have them, also to how to make their products safer.

"We have the smart gun technology that's been commercially ready for some time to be able to have a fingerprint scanner on there or make sure only those intended to use the firearm and who are trained to use it have access to it. They ought to support locks to make sure that children don't get their hands on firearms.

"My wife and I have two young kids, and when they want to go to friends' houses, we ask parents if they have firearms in the house, and if so, if they are locked. If they say no, we don't let the kids go. I'm not exactly bashful. It ought to be the de facto thing that every parent does to make sure guns are locked away.

"I'm a perennial optimist. I think the American people are better than this President. I believe that to my core. We've seen an unprecedented dishonesty and corruption, and it's time to move on, back to a President we can be proud of again, with integrity and decency. With regard to gun violence, it's clear nothing will change until we have leaders who will take a stand and have meaningful reform in the White House and Congress. I think in 2020, we will put someone there who will prevent future tragedies, and I will fight really hard to ensure that's the case."

Parents and politicians alike are shouldering this burden of attempting to eradicate gun violence, in a range of different ways. People discuss gun violence mostly as either Democrats or Republicans; they see red or blue. But my authoritative title, the one on my nametag, is "*Dad.*" I am Jesse and Jaime's dad. I see orange. I understand that gun violence is not partisan. I understand that when bullets hit you, they do not know if you are Republican or Democrat, red or blue, rich or poor, or what color you are. I understand that when bullets hit, they are likely to kill. Because I am Jesse and Jaime's dad, I plan to work with everyone possible to solve this.

Chapter 15

Dreams and Dedication

Dreams and dedication

When I set out to write this book, my original intention was simply to tell my story. However, as I began writing, it became clear to me that telling my story is not possible without all of the amazing and inspiring people who have been a part of it. My story would not have been possible without all of the helpers who were part of my life before Jaime was murdered and those who became a part of my life after. What I have learned is that it is the helpers who carried me. It is the helpers who helped me to move forward. It is the helpers who gave me inspiration and who lifted me when I was weak. It is the helpers who encouraged me through the negativity that accompanied my mission. We all suffer amazing highs and lows in life. My ultimate advice to anyone is that whatever you are going through, always seek out your helpers. They are there, and they will carry you when you need it.

As I write this final chapter, this country is in the middle of the coronavirus pandemic. As you read this, I truly hope that this idea of relying on helpers is something that you find useful. Helpers may be family. They may be people in media that you come to rely upon. They may be politicians that you rely on for information. They may be friends who simply organize online video sessions so that you can all stay connected. We all have our helpers, and learning to embrace them is a way through both our best moments in life and also our hardest and darkest moments.

Over the past two years, I have had the great fortune of meeting many people who I now consider heroes. None of them could ever have achieved what they did without the helpers in their lives. I have learned from them how to rely on others while pursuing my mission, and because of these helpful others, we will succeed.

Jaime had a favorite saying for which she was known and by which she lived her life: "Dreams and dedication are a powerful combination." While she found this quote online, it defined her. Through this inspirational quote, my little girl helps to motivate me and push me forward every day. She is my ultimate helper. I have a dream of a country where we work together to reduce gun violence. and I am dedicating the rest of my life to making sure that it happens. However, while I am highly visible and may look purposeful as I pursue my mission, the reality is that I do have many bad days—days where I have a hard time pushing myself forward. On days like that, I look to Jaime for inspiration and sometimes to others as well.

On August 27, 2019, I woke up to a Facebook memory and realized it had been three years that day since Jaime's bat mitzvah.

One of the ways that I get through bad moments and steady myself, as I needed to do that day, is to put on Billy Joel. His music has simply meant more to me throughout my life than that of any other musician. I kid you not, in the days and weeks following February 14, 2018, I would actually just go for a drive to be by myself and listen to Billy Joel. He is another person (though he does not know it) who has helped me through this!

About two months after Jaime was killed, I put a message on Twitter about how Billy Joel's music helps me and thanking him for it. Several musicians from his original band now play in a group called The Lords of 52nd Street. Their manager saw my message and reached out. They still perform, and we have since met with them several times. It is moments like this, happening when I need them most, that continue to remind me that my faith in people is well placed, and that because of the phenomenal people who continue to come into my life, I will be okay.

I always used to tell my wife and kids that as long as we wake up in the morning and those we love and care about are safe and healthy and go to sleep at night and everyone is still safe and healthy, that it was a good day. Everything else in between was just a bunch of stuff that we had to manage and get through. I try to hold onto this belief while still being realistic about what we lost. Truth is, we have had really bad days lately. My life now is one of finding a path forward for my wife, for my son, and for myself. We have to do this while dealing daily with the reality of what we miss. Our home is very different.

It is much quieter.

In fact, at Jaime's funeral, I spoke about what her voice meant to us:

> Your family and friends who lived for your voice
> and spirit will not feel it ever again. It will be
> different. Your humor, your craziness, your energy,
> and your feistiness will be missed. My baby girl,
> you were the energy in our house. You were the
> energy in every room that you went into. Our
> new normal will be a lot quieter. I will miss the
> sounds of your laughter, your unbelievable ability
> to never stop talking, and how quickly you would
> say things because you always had so much to say.
> They were the sounds that gave our life meaning
> and our house energy. Jaime, you loved life, you
> were the energy in the room, you made your
> presence known.

This is the reality of what we miss. Every day we are trying to find our new normal. Since Jaime's murder, the people I've met, the places I've gone, and the things that have happened are nothing short of unbelievable. But there is no sense of fame or excitement about it. My mission and purpose drive me, not the excitement of meeting people. For me, the truth is just like what Mr. Rogers said in that famous quote, "Always look for the helpers. There will always be helpers." Everyone with whom I have come in contact, everyone who has been a part of my life or become a part of my life, they are all my helpers. With helpers in our life, there is hope.

Every day I wake up unsure of how I am going to feel that day, what with not having my complete family anymore, and some days, like today, I think I am okay. But that feeling can change in a minute. Maybe it's because I didn't travel one week and I'm not worn out, or maybe it's because I did travel and finished the week feeling drained. You just never know when you are going to feel okay or when you are going to need help from others to feel that way. There are days where I wake up and just can't get my head going.

Sometimes I will spend moments, hours, or the entire day just looking at pictures or video or driving to the cemetery to sit with Jaime. This grief is unpredictable and sometimes unexplainable. Life has become a series of firsts: first birthday celebrations without Jaime, first holidays without Jaime, watching friends of Jaime's have their sweet sixteen parties and their first loves. Every day is a first. Those Facebook memories come up every day and trigger these loops: the graduation we are not planning; the car we are not buying; the wedding for which I don't get to walk my daughter down the aisle.

I recently was asked the question, "How would you characterize your experience when your brother Michael died compared to changes in you after Jaime died? How did these different losses affect you?"

I went from a level of sadness that I had thought was the worst possible to one that was a thousand times worse. After my brother died, my focus got small. I focused first on Jen and the kids, and then on what I was going to do, as I had sold my business previously and no longer had to go back and forth to New York to take care of my brother. But when Jaime died, that circle burst. All I think about now is what I can do on behalf of 40,000 people a year: the victims of gun violence. It is all-consuming.

The biggest shift is not looking ahead anymore. I do not have a long-term view. It's one day at a time. The reality is that I now understand that life can change in a second, and nothing is more important to me than what is happening right now. Every day, surrounded by the love and support of my helpers both near and far, I make the best of that day. On the next day, we start over.

When I was a teenager, my aunt once said to me that life is not a straight path, it is like a drive on a winding and hilly road. There will be many highs and many lows, and many curves. We will also hit potholes and speed bumps along the way. Sometimes, we won't be sure where to turn or how to move forward. However, she told me to always continue going forward and encouraged me, telling me that I would always find my way. Looking back on my life, she was right. I have had an amazing life, filled with wonderful highs and challenging lows. What losing Jaime has taught me, perhaps by reinforcing what I had already learned, are the lessons of perspective. I have been happily married to the same person now for twenty-one years, and the two best days of my life were the days when my two children were born. I have been unemployed and not known how I would pay the bills, and then had an amazing corporate career in sales and sales management. I have been a business owner with the many highs and lows that go with that. What I can say with certainty is that none of it comes close to what I am experiencing now. My prior worst moments do not compare. *My hope is that from stories like mine, we can all learn the lesson of perspective: that you have levels of strength and resilience of which you are unaware until you are tested.*

Remember my story when you are going through what seems like a bad moment or the worst moment in school, on the job, in business, or in life. And then think about all of the other moments before when you felt that same way, and remember that they passed—they became nothing more than a memory followed by amazing new moments. Remember that you got through it. I believe that there are moments in life that are so significant that when they come, they're not just challenges, but opportunities for greatness. In this journey of mine as a gun safety advocate, I have met great people, heroes, who fought back after tragedy, just like I met heroes who came out of the 9/11 tragedy.

What I learned from my brother, who hid out in the basement of one of the towers of the World Trade Center while it collapsed on him and then followed that by spending the next sixteen days treating people, or what I have learned from the many gun violence prevention warriors whose relationships and friendships I now rely upon, who do what they do because of gun violence, is that it is in life's hardest moments that our country's heroes and leaders are born. I am thankful for the many heroes I have met. They have become my helpers, and I hope that I can be a helper to you.

To anyone who reads this book, especially the kids and young adults, and to the future leaders and heroes, you will have many moments in your life, some bigger than others. Ultimately, what matters more than the moment is how you respond to it. How you react to your moment when it comes is what will define you.

Acknowledgments

There are many significant people who played a part in making this book a reality. It would not have been possible without the two people I loved who will never get the chance to read this book. They are my daughter, Jaime, and my brother, Michael.

I have had the great fortune of connecting with so many wonderful people who have made an impact on my life that trying to name them all will be impossible; and I am worried that if I try to list them, I will leave someone out. Instead, just let me thank my amazing family: my mom and dad, Marvin and Ethel Guttenberg; my mother-in-law and father-in-law, Steve and Joan Bloom; my siblings, Abbie Youkilis and her family, Ira Guttenberg and his family, and Paul Guttenberg and his family; as well as my brother- and sister-in-law, Erik and Stacie Bloom, and their kids. Aunts, uncles, and cousins have also lived through this with us. Of course, I must also thank my amazing long-time and dear friends who have all stood by my side as I pursued my advocacy. I have friends who lived through the loss of my daughter and brother with me, some in unbelievably deep and meaningful ways. You are family to me. Many have had concerns about my safety and often about my sanity, yet they were a constant source of encouragement and support as I have continued to fight for gun safety and write this book.

Following the murder of my daughter and the death of my brother, amazing people who were never a part of my life before entered it. Whether I met each of them through my brother's network of friends and colleagues, or through the murder of my daughter, I am thankful to all of the politicians, entertainers, and amazing new friends who have helped me, encouraged me, and inspired me. My life is fuller for having gotten to know all of you.

To all of those who agreed to be interviewed for this book, thank you! Thank you for allowing me to tell how you inspired me, helped me, and encouraged me. Thank you for being a part of my life, or my family's life, in such a meaningful way. This book would not have been possible without your involvement.

Thank you, Candi Cross, my collaborative writer, who has worked with me on this book project from the very beginning to include interviews, organization, and chapter development. She treated my story as though it was the most important project in the world. She helped me to make this book a success as we developed the pages to tell my brother's story, my daughter's story, and how they both changed me and pushed me into this world of fighting for gun safety. Together, we were able to capture my story in a meaningful and complete way. Her insights and expertise added much to this project. I hope those who read it will feel the emotion that is a part of my life, but also be inspired by my advocacy to do bigger things.

I want to thank my editor, Jenna Land Free, who helped me to bring out new meanings and pushed me to go deeper into places that I did not at first want to go. Her work with me has ensured that this book and its purpose around finding helpers will hopefully have more depth and meaning to others who read it.

Thank you to my book agent, Howard Yoon, who believed in my book and worked with me to ensure that it would be published. He also is the creative mind who, after reading my book, said this book is all about helpers and helped me to bring my story to this place. He also introduced me to my editor Jenna. Howard, thank you for believing in me and for helping me to reach this final product. Because of you, I believe this is a book that not only tells my story but will also be a road map for others who are going through grief and who need helpers.

Thank you to Mango Publishing for understanding my vision and for publishing my book. I am truly grateful to have you and your team of amazing helpers in my life as I tell my story and hopefully help others in need.

Most importantly, thank you to my wife, Jennifer, and my son, Jesse. Our life has not been easy since we lost Jaime. We have all changed. I have not always been easy to be around as the emotion of our loss has changed me. My focus used to be purely on what was happening in our home. Now, I am on this mission that puts me into a very public and political place. This is not a place that either my wife or my son asked for or desired. I know that, and I am beyond thankful to them for standing by my side. I am thankful to them for their strength and encouragement at a time when we are all struggling on this path of redefining who we are as a family. I am thankful to them for allowing me to pursue and write this book. For me, writing is very healing, and writing this book has helped me. I love them with every ounce of my being.

Afterword

Most people are familiar with the stages of grief. These include denial, anger, bargaining, depression, and acceptance. What most don't realize until they go through their own set of circumstances related to loss is that everyone goes through grief differently, in their own way, in their own time. For some, grief is very private. For others, it is a way to connect with those who have been through a similar situation. Yet for some rare individuals, it sparks a fight in them to make sure that nobody else has to ever feel the way that they do. As you now know from reading Fred's book, he is a fighter.

There we were, in the denial phase. How could it be? How could my daughter be gone? She had less than a 1 percent chance of being a victim, but she was. She was the first one to be plastered all over the news. Pictures were taken from social media without our permission. Media was stationed in front of our home for days. We had no time to think, to digest the situation, to begin to grieve. The city kicked into full gear, holding vigils, town halls, and so on. Fred was asked to speak, and our new life began. No longer were we just community members; we were now "those people."

I sat home paralyzed, but at the same time trying to comfort our family, our friends, and Jaime's friends. I was so thankful my son survived, but I also knew that being part of this horrific tragedy would affect him for the rest of his life. Jaime's name and face became known nationally and even internationally. It was surreal.

Fred has always had fight in him, standing up for what he believes in. As a pediatric occupational therapist, I have always been a helper, caring for others before dealing with myself. It was only fitting that Fred would use his voice to stand up for our daughter and the sixteen others that didn't make it out that day, and I would try to help others get through their pain and loss along with mine.

With his national presence, Fred was able to begin standing up for EVERY person ever affected by gun violence in any form. I began to immediately make sure Jaime's kind, giving, and compassionate soul lived on by giving back to causes and organizations that were important to her. I had our family and friends help us to keep her name alive by volunteering for our organization so they could feel like they had the ability to stay connected to her in the most positive way. Kids and adults alike learned to be more caring and giving. This is what Jaime taught people. All people. And we will never let that stop. She was a helper when she was here with us, working with kids and teens with special needs. She was always there for her friends whenever they needed her. Jaime was also the best daughter and taught us so many lessons in her short time on Earth. We had to let that continue.

Michael was also a helper. He saved many lives by risking his own. He ran into danger when others were running out. He did this his whole life. Although he never wanted accolades, he was our hero. Thank goodness he survived on 9/11, but he succumbed to his illness later due to his time spent helping others.

Life is not always fair. We have learned that the hard way in such a short amount of time, starting in October 2017 and again in Feb 2018. What we have also learned is that there are so many ways to respond to adversity and tragedy. Fred and I have definitely gone through our grieving processes very differently. He won't stop until he's done everything he can to get the change this country so desperately needs. I won't stop honoring my daughter's beautiful outlook on life and her determination to change the world. She truly wanted to make it a better place with inclusion for ALL.

Although we are different, our hearts are in the same place. I fully support Fred and agree with what he fights for. I help when I can from the sidelines. He fully supports me in working with the people and organizations that meant so much to Jaime and helps me too. Michael was an American hero and we both talk about him and will always portray him as such. First responders are some of the most important people in our communities, and they risk their lives daily at the expense of helping others.

Fred and I have both found our helpers throughout this process. He has taught me many good lessons. His famous phrase to the kids was "always do what's right," and we will continue to follow that for the rest of our lives. It is certainly not always easy, but we care too much about others to stop. Jaime and Michael inspired us every day and continue to do so. Their legacies must live on.

This book ends with a small directory of helpers, organizations, and nonprofits whose purpose is to uplift, support, and offer real help to those in need. These are just a few of so many across the world. We want you to know that no matter what you have been through, there are always helpers. They may be right there beside you or you may have to seek them out, but they are there. From Fred Roger's educational programs for kids to charities for animals, we encourage you to check them all out. In addition, there are so many others that you can find for yourselves with a click of the mouse.

We would also love to hear from you. Who has helped you in your life? What are your ideas of what we can do to make this a better world? Please keep in touch with us. As the photo here illustrates, now is the time for us to join together and become a community of kindness that stands up for and with others.

Please follow Orange Ribbons for Jaime on Facebook, Instagram, and Twitter. Go to our website orangeribbonsforjaime.org to see what our foundation is up to and sign up for email updates. Email us at info@orangeribbonsmail.org.

As the wise and wonderful Fred Rogers said, "Always look for the helpers. There will always be helpers." Both Fred and I thank you for taking the time to read this book. We hope you walk away inspired, motivated, and ready to do your part for what you believe in. Who knows? Maybe one day without even realizing it, you will be considered someone else's helper.

JENNIFER GUTTENBERG

Finding Helpers Resource

Orange Ribbons for Jaime
orangeribbonsforjaime.org
Orange Ribbons for Jaime was founded by Fred and Jennifer
Guttenberg after losing his daughter Jaime in the Parkland
shooting. The foundation focuses on supporting groups that
Jaime was passionate about helping (The Humane Society,
Jacob's Pillow, The Friendship Journey, and the Paley Institute)
as well as educate others and push for common-sense gun laws.

The Friendship Journey
thefriendshipjourney.org
The Friendship Journey's inclusive programs provide
opportunities for children, teens, and young adults of all physical
and cognitive abilities to enjoy extracurricular activities while
forming authentic connections.

Kindness.org Non Profit
kindness.org/about
Using education and research, kindness.org aims to use acts of
kindness as a catalyst for change. Their mission is to make a more
kind world.

Random Acts of Kindness Foundation
randomactsofkindness.org
Spreading videos and resources of acts of kindness to help inspire
others to do the same. Also is helping spread positive activities to
do during COVID-19.

Brady Campaign to End Gun Violence
bradyunited.org
Brady campaign is named after the bipartisan Brady law passed
in 1993. The goal of the campaign is to address gun violence

in America as a unique issue and try to end gun violence from
all angles.

Newtown Action Alliance
newtownactionalliance.org

Newton Action Alliance was formed after the Sandy Hook
elementary school shooting. They work to have legislative
changes in local, state, and federal levels. They also lobby for
cultural changes to end gun violence and has links to donate and
volunteer. Every December they hold a vigil in Washington, DC,
for all survivors and families affected by gun violence.

Giffords Law Center
lawcenter.giffords.org

Congresswoman Gabrielle Gillford was shot in 2011, and from
that formed this foundation to end gun violence through policy
and legislation. They also help fund federal research as well as
educate others on gun violence.

Kindness Rocks Project
thekindnessrocksproject.com

Founded by empowering life coach Megan Murphy, The
Kindness Rocks Projects was founded to encourage people to
leave inspiring messages painted on rocks. This impacts others to
practice spreading kindness in a tactical way.

David Bohnett Foundation
bohnettfoundation.org/programs/gun-violence-prevention

Founded by philanthropist David Bohnett, the foundation
provides grants to help fund and research a wide variety of topics
that require social activism, including gun violence.

Sandy Hook Promise Foundation
sandyhookpromise.org

The Sandy Hook Promise Foundation aims to honor gun

violence victims by supporting and protecting policies that look at the human side of gun violence. The goal is to protect children from gun violence by also preventing individuals to use firearms for harming themselves or others.

City of Kindness
cityofkindness.org
A coalition of organizations wanting to spread kindness in our world. Their website provides resources to inspire being kind to others.

Everyday Kindness
everyday-kindness.secure.force.com
Everyday kindness works with schools to develop programs to inspire kindness between students, as an act to end violence and bullying.

Think Kindness
thinkkindness.org
Works to spread measurable acts of kindness in schools across the country. Also tours schools in fifteen days to inspire through speakers and presentations.

Spreadkindness.org
spreadkindness.org/about
Nonprofit that aims to spread kindness through individuals and groups by passing on, inspiring, and enlightening acts of joy.

National Alliance on Mental Illness
nami.org/About-Mental-Illness/Mental-Health-Conditions/Posttraumatic-Stress-Disorder
Provides information, treatment, and support for mental illness including depression, PTSD, and anxiety.

The Dougy Center
dougy.org/about-us
The Dougy Center provides a place for grieving children, teens, and their families to share their experience and hopefully heal.

Compassionate Friends
compassionatefriends.org
Compassionate friends is a self-help organization that provides support and hope to grieving families after losing a child.

Kids for Peace
kidsforpeaceglobal.org
Organization that empowers youth through service and thoughtful acts of kindness.

World Kindness Movement
theworldkindnessmovement.org
This is a global nonprofit that is thought of as the head of kindness movements globally. The mission of the WKM is to inspire individuals towards greater kindness by connecting nations to create a kinder world.

Charter for Compassion
charterforcompassion.org/about1/about-overview
The charter for compassion is a network that wants to inspire everyone to live under the principle of compassion through connecting organizers and leaders from around the world, providing educational resources, organizing tools, and avenues for communication.

Eagles Haven
eagleshaven.org
Eagles Haven is located in Parkland, Florida. They are a community wellness center created solely and mindfully for the MSD/Eagles community following the shooting in Parkland.

They provide current, future, and former students, family members, and faculty one representative and nurturing place to call or drop in for any supportive service or wellness needs.

Voices of 9/11
voicesofsept11.org

A wonderful group for those who have been through 9/11 and need a helpful resource.

Humane Society
humanesociety.org

The Humane Society takes on puppy mills, factory farms, the fur trade, trophy hunting, animal cosmetics testing, and other cruel industries. They rescue and care for thousands of animals every year through their Animal Rescue Team's work and other hands-on animal care services. They fight all forms of animal cruelty to achieve the vision behind the organization's name: A humane society.

Hospice
Vitas.com

Hospice is a type of medical care that gives seriously ill patients and their loved ones meaningful time together when the focus of care turns from active treatment to comfort and quality of life near the end of life. Hospice is not a place. Rather, it is a full range of services that put patients and families in control, giving them hope about their last days, weeks and months together.

Fred Rogers Productions
www.fredrogers.org

Fred Rogers Productions builds on the legacy of Fred Rogers by creating quality children's media that models an enthusiasm for learning and earns the trust of parents and caregivers. We believe it's never too early for kids to discover the fun of following their curiosity, while they learn meaningful life skills along the way.

About the Author

Fred Guttenberg's professional life includes over a decade of experience in sales and management with Johnson & Johnson, followed by almost fifteen years as an entrepreneur, having built a business consisting of multiple Dunkin' Donuts locations in Florida and Tennessee, which he sold in November 2016. Fred was hoping to take some time to relax before getting involved in real estate and looking for other opportunities. Then tragedy struck.

Fred's brother, Michael, one of the original first responders on 9/11 at the World Trade Center, was trapped with a team of doctors at the bottom of one of the towers as it collapsed. Amazingly, the room where they hid out did not collapse, and Michael and his team of physicians spent sixteen days at Ground Zero taking care of others. As a result of the Ground Zero exposure, Michael was diagnosed with pancreatic cancer, which he battled with the help of Fred and other family members and friends until October 2017, when he passed away.

Following Michael's funeral, Fred, who was understandably still trying to recover from the passing of his brother, also recognized he needed something else to do. In February of 2018, Fred was actively looking for a new life purpose when he and his family were struck by another national American tragedy; only this one was in many ways far worse. His fourteen-year-old daughter, Jaime, a freshman at Marjory Stoneman Douglas High School, was one of seventeen victims brutally murdered in the Parkland, Florida, school shooting.

From that day forward, Fred's life would be forever changed. While grieving, Fred found himself unable to stand still. The day after the murder, he attended a vigil in Parkland; and while there, he was asked to speak. That was the start of a new public life for Fred. He was angry and quickly realized his purpose as an American advocate in the fight for public safety.

Fred now spends time challenging our elected officials and business leaders to do more and is aggressively pursuing strategies to enhance public safety, enact common sense gun safety, and turn out the vote through his nonprofit organization dedicated to Jaime's life, Orange Ribbons for Jaime, and his nonprofit organization dedicated to advocacy, Orange Ribbons For Gun Safety. He has been a regular on TV news programs and myriad print and online media outlets. Through the formation of the nonprofits, this is Fred's fulltime mission. His leadership and perseverance—despite these dual tragedies—is awe-inspiring, and his ability to turn the worst possible grief into action and to attain ongoing results is nationally known.

Fred Guttenberg moved to Florida from Long Island in 1989, shortly after graduating from Skidmore College in New York. Fred, his wife, Jennifer, and their son, Jesse, currently reside in Parkland, Florida.

Mango Publishing, established in 2014, publishes an eclectic list of books by diverse authors—both new and established voices—on topics ranging from business, personal growth, women's empowerment, LGBTQ studies, health, and spirituality to history, popular culture, time management, decluttering, lifestyle, mental wellness, aging, and sustainable living. We were recently named 2019's #1 fastest growing independent publisher by *Publishers Weekly*. Our success is driven by our main goal, which is to publish high quality books that will entertain readers as well as make a positive difference in their lives.

Our readers are our most important resource; we value your input, suggestions, and ideas. We'd love to hear from you—after all, we are publishing books for you!

Please stay in touch with us and follow us at:

Facebook: Mango Publishing
Twitter: @MangoPublishing
Instagram: @MangoPublishing
LinkedIn: Mango Publishing
Pinterest: Mango Publishing

Sign up for our newsletter at www.mangopublishinggroup.com and receive a free book!

Join us on Mango's journey to reinvent publishing, one book at a time.